THE HSI MOVEMENT

THE HSI MOVEMENT

STRATEGIES DRIVING CHANGE AT HISPANIC-SERVING INSTITUTIONS

GINA ANN GARCIA

JOHNS HOPKINS UNIVERSITY PRESS | *Baltimore*

 Published 2026
First printed in the United States of America on acid-free paper
2 4 6 8 9 7 5 3 1

Johns Hopkins University Press
2715 North Charles Street
Baltimore, Maryland 21218
www.press.jhu.edu

Library of Congress Cataloging-in-Publication Data is available.

A catalog record for this book is available from the British Library.
ISBN 978-1-4214-5549-5 (paperback)
ISBN 978-1-4214-5550-1 (ebook)

EU GPSR Authorized Representative
LOGOS EUROPE, 9 rue Nicolas Poussin, 17000, La Rochelle, France
E-mail: contact@logoseurope.eu

To the grassroots leaders, changemakers, and organizers
in the HSI movement.
¡Que viva el movimiento!

CONTENTS

ACKNOWLEDGMENTS

Writing is a privilege. And I am grateful for the opportunity to be a thought leader in the HSI movement, using my voice to motivate our grassroots leaders, changemakers, and organizers.

I must acknowledge the 32 educators who agreed to share their stories with me through the research study titled "HSIs in Transition." This book would not be possible without you. I wish I could name each and every one of you here, but as a researcher I have vowed to protect your identity. But you know who you are, and I do too. I am grateful you trusted me with your story and allowed me to share it with other educators, leaders, and organizers in the HSI movement.

I also want to note that 21 of my participants are Latina-identified women. This is important because I see Latinas leading the HSI work on many campuses. Yet we know Latinas continue to be underpaid, and oftentimes the HSI work is undercompensated and underacknowledged. Many Latinas do this work because it is heart work, and they do it with their full corazón because they care about Latine students, families, and communities. So I would be remiss if I didn't shout out the Latina-identified women in the HSI movement.

I want to give flowers to my summer 2022 writing group, Los Girasoles: Marialexia Zaragoza, Esteban Alcalá, Emily Koren, Maribel Jiménez, Desiree "Dez" Zuniga, Julianna Hernandez, Arlene Cano-Matute, Brandi Windham, Ariel Stevenson, Christina Ryan Rodriguez, and Sasha Villagrana-Frost. I conceptualized the "HSIs in Transition" study, wrote the proposal for this book, submitted the IRB application for the data collection, and developed the protocol during our weekly writing sessions. Thank you for holding me accountable to writing and research, and for sharing space that summer. We were together when 19 students and two teachers were fatally shot in Uvalde, TX, and we held space when the Supreme Court overturned Roe v. Wade. It was a memorable summer, and we held each other close, knowing our writing group was a brave space where we could connect, network, vent, cry, and of course write. We also found joy in music, as Bad Bunny released *Un Verano Sin Ti* that summer, which became our soundtrack.

I must also recognize my graduate students Marialexia Zaragoza, Esteban Alcalá, and Nathaly Santos, who each contributed to *The HSI Movement* in different ways throughout the lifecycle of the study. Nathaly did some heavy lifting as a PhD student, helping me code the 32 manuscripts and running preliminary analysis guided by the emergent strategy framework. I am forever thankful.

There are others who made *The HSI Movement* possible, like Rich Milner, who has no idea how he influenced this book, but thank you, Rich. Estefanía Toledo, who is amazing in so many ways, helped to promote the study on my website and through social media—gracias!

And to my editor at Johns Hopkins University Press, Greg Britton, thank you for helping me to complete the trilogy. I appreciate everyone at the Press who continues to support me with each book.

THE HSI MOVEMENT

INTRODUCTION

Hispanic Serving Institutions in Transition

THE HSI COMMUNITY HAS ENTERED what I call the "transitional era," leaving behind what I term the "enrollment era." The enrollment era lasted approximately 26 years (1992–2018) and was symbolized by *enrollment*, with Hispanic Serving Institutions (HSIs) defined in federal legislation as not-for-profit, degree-granting colleges and universities whose enrollment is at least 25% Hispanic students. The HSI designation was officially acknowledged with the reauthorization of the Higher Education Act (HEA) in 1992 and amended to Title III (Valdez, 2015). The HSI legislation was funded in 1995 and moved to Title V of the HEA in 1998, officially launching a new institutional type that was legitimized and competitively funded by the federal government.

The enrollment era was also signified by *eligibility*, with HSI status confirmed by the Department of Education based on (1) the number of "needy students," or those who receive Pell grants, federal supplemental educational opportunity grants (SEOG), federal work study, and federal Perkins loans; (2) the minimum percentage of students from specific racial or ethnic backgrounds, which is 25% for HSIs; and (3) the campus core expenses per full-time equivalent enrollment (US Department of Education, n.d.). The Department of Education provides HSIs with an eligibility letter, enabling them to apply for competitive funding to address the educational needs of Latine students.

A third dimension of the enrollment era was *grants*. During the 26 years of the enrollment era, approximately 520 institutions met the criteria, with many pursuing eligibility and applying for HSI grants. The Department of Education administers two discretionary grant programs earmarked for HSIs, falling under Title V, Part A (Developing Hispanic-Serving Institutions [DHSI] Program) and Title V, Part B (Promoting Postbaccalaureate Opportunities for Hispanic Americans [PPOHA] Program), as well as one mandatory grant program under Title III, Part F (Hispanic-Serving Institutions—Science, Technology, Engineering, or Mathematics and Articulation [HSI STEM] Program). These programs were collectively allocated $349 million in FY23, and nearly $4.5 billion has been disbursed to HSIs through these programs since 1995 (Hispanic Association of Colleges and Universities [HACU], 2024). This investment is monumental and an important marker of federal commitment to HSIs. During the enrollment era, many colleges and universities applied for and received HSI grants, enabling them to launch projects that support Latine students' access and success. Aguilar-Smith and Yun (2023) found that from 2009 to 2017, 339 unique institutions applied for Title V grants, representing 70% of eligible institutions. In other words, a majority of eligible HSIs applied, and most applied more than once (Aguilar-Smith & Yun, 2023).

While enrollment, eligibility, and grants are crucial to the HSI community, these markers do not define a Latine-serving identity. In fact, these dimensions are the epitome of a Latine-*enrolling* identity: We *enroll* 25% Hispanic students, we are *eligible* for federal grants, and we seek (and sometimes get) HSI *grants* (Garcia, 2017a). For most of us in the HSI community, being Latine-enrolling is simply not enough. We want to see dramatic change to the institutions that have historically harmed and excluded Latine students. Yet the enrollment era mostly encouraged first-order change, or what is generally referred to as minor tweaks and adjustments, facilitated by HSI grants with little accountability for institutionalizing change efforts or advancing true transformation. Title V grant abstracts reveal that a majority of these tweaks were programmatic with no real plan for second-order change, or the disruption of the deep-seated culture for educating students. Otherwise stated, wraparound support programs cannot shift the institutional logics for serving Latine students. HSIs must change the values, assumptions, processes, and policies for serving an underserved racial-ethnic group, which will require a paradigm shift.

The Transitional Era

There were several rupture points in 2019 that moved us into what I call the "transitional era" (2019–), including the publication of the Multidimensional Conceptual Framework for Understanding Servingness at HSIs ("the servingness framework"; Garcia et al., 2019a) and the launching of the Seal of Excelencia (a data-driven certification created by Excelencia in Education), both of which provided the HSI community with frameworks for organizational change. I argue that the transitional era is marked by intentional efforts to become HSIs beyond enrollment, eligibility, and grant seeking and getting. It is demarcated by organizational change as campuses lean in to doing something different with and for their Latine students. HSIs in transition are actively moving from Latine-enrolling, or simply meeting the federal enrollment and eligibility requirements, to Latine-serving, which I have envisioned as an organizational identity that embodies equitable outcomes and experiences for Latine people and an institutional culture that centers the identities, histories, lived experiences, and community cultural wealth of Latines (Garcia, 2017a, 2017b, 2019). HSIs in transition have embraced the concept of servingness, which is a commitment to Latine student success beyond enrollment, reflective assessment of processes and practices, data-driven decision-making, structural transformation, advancement of equitable academic and liberatory outcomes, and collective action

(Garcia et al., 2019a). HSIs in transition are challenging the institutional logics that have harmed Latine students and instead are creating spaces for educational liberation and justice.

HSIs in transition are becoming "HSI-minded," which I define as an awareness of HSI scholarship and best practices and a strong commitment to proactively disrupting a Latine-enrolling, HSI-eligible, grant-seeking identity. The campus collectively becomes HSI-minded as educators and students engage in a process of HSI knowledge acquisition, staying up-to-date on HSI empirical research and accessing other critical theoretical perspectives such as community cultural wealth, critical whiteness, decolonial theory, and anti-Blackness. HSI-minded campuses host book clubs on campus and sponsor day-long HSI symposia where folks engage in critical conversations about servingness and provide HSI-specific training and professional development. To become HSI-minded is to fundamentally shift the view of HSIs as more than enrolling, eligible, and grant-seeking institutions and to engage in a process of learning the unique histories, background, lived experiences, and ways of knowing of Latine students. Yet to become HSI-minded is a process, or what Villarreal (2022) calls a "path to conocimiento of servingness." (p. 9).

In addition to already eligible HSIs, HSIs in transition include emerging HSIs (eHSIs) that enroll between 15% and 24% Latine students. Although this is not an official designation and does not make campuses eligible for funding, the term "emerging HSIs" was coined by Excelencia in Education (2010) and has been embraced by researchers and practitioners to indicate that a campus is moving toward the 25% enrollment. HSIs in transition also include campuses I call "striving HSIs" (sHSIs), which are colleges and universities below 15% Latine enrollment. I call these institutions "striving HSIs" because they are actively working toward the 25% enrollment and making organizational changes while doing it. Some of them have adopted servingness practices, launched HSI task forces, and started building HSI awareness on campus. At some of these striving HSIs, I've given public lectures on servingness to a room full of faculty, staff, and administrators who want to intentionally prepare the campus for the arrival of more Latine students. I have not published anything to date that defines "striving HSIs," but I have experienced these campuses and know firsthand that they meet my definition of "HSIs in transition." Arguably, we can learn a lot from eHSIs and sHSIs (and we do in this book).

The transitional era is symbolized by what I call "the HSI movement." Drawing on research by sociologists Mayer Zald and Michael Berger, I argue that the HSI movement is inclusive of educators and grassroots leaders who are committed to changing behaviors, goals, policies, and practices within the colleges and universities that meet the 25% enrollment and eligibility requirements to be HSIs (Garcia, 2023, November 20). The HSI movement dates back to 1976 when Latine advocates in Washington, DC, began lobbying for increased funding to support institutions enrolling the largest percentage of Latine students (Valdez, 2015). There have since been many milestones in the movement, including the establishment of HACU in 1986, the founding of the Alliance for Hispanic Serving Institution Educators (AHSIE) in 2007, the establishment of ESCALA Educational Services in 2013, the launching of the Seal of Excelencia in 2019, the introduction of *¿Qué pasa, HSIs?* (the podcast dedicated to all things HSIs) in 2021, and the start of the Alliance of Hispanic Serving Research Universities in 2022. With each of these milestones we have seen growth in the number of educators, advocates, and supporters of HSIs, transforming it from a small group of dedicated individuals to a mass movement.

As the movement gains momentum, we are witnessing substantial change in policies and practices across HSIs. The organizers in the HSI movement are sharing best practices, publishing journal articles and policy briefs, posting on their HSI-specific social media accounts, and talking about their work on *¿Qué pasa, HSIs?* They are accessing their external resources; they attend the AHSIE and HACU conferences to share and learn about HSI best practices; they tap into programs sponsored by Excelencia in Education and apply for the Seal of Excelencia; and they send faculty and administrator cohorts to trainings offered by ESCALA Educational Services.

We are seeing more HSIs prioritize servingness in their strategic plans, launch an HSI task force, and hire an HSI director. Some states now have HSI consortia (or similar groups) to support the HSIs in their region, including Arizona, Colorado, Texas, Massachusetts, and Wisconsin, with each accessing diverse resources to mobilize HSI efforts. We are also witnessing the emergence of student-led movements, with campuses launching student HSI advisory committees, student HSI teams, and HSI-specific undergraduate research opportunities. HSI organizers are unapologetic in their efforts and challenging the way we have historically served Latine students, calling for a different approach to educating and empowering students.

To be clear, some HSIs continue to define themselves strictly by enrollment, eligibility, and grants. But for those HSIs that have embraced transition, the impact of the threats to HSIs under the 47th president of the United States is less severe. On September 10, 2025, the Department of Education announced it would end $350 million in discretionary funding to enrollment-based Minority Serving Institutions (MSIs) including HSIs, Asian American and Native American Pacific Islander Serving Institutions (AANAPISI), Predominantly Black Institutions (PBI), Native American Serving Nontribal Institutions (NASNTI), and Alaska Native and Native Hawaiian Serving Institutions (ANNHSI) (Weissman, September 11, 2025). This followed a lawsuit filed in June 2025 by the State of Tennessee and Students for Fair Admissions asserting that HSIs are discriminatory (Weissman, June 13, 2025). While the case has not gone to court and enrollment-based MSIs are still codified in the HEA, the Department of Education under the 47th president of the United States will no longer fund discretionary grant programs for enrollment-based institutions, putting them in limbo. The loss of discretionary funding is a devastating blow to HSIs, but it is not the end of them. HSIs in transition know that enrollment, eligibility, and grants do not define them, and they will continue to engage in organizational change toward servingness.

The History and Role of HSI Research

The HSI movement is fueled by written knowledge about HSIs, which is crucial to becoming HSI-minded. Research during the *enrollment era* laid a foundation for what it means to be Latine-enrolling, HSI eligible, and HSI grantees—not necessarily Latine-serving—and provided an understanding of (1) the definition, history, and evolution of HSIs; (2) the significance of HSIs; (3) the major challenges and barriers facing HSIs; (4) the contextual effects of HSIs on student experiences and outcomes; and (5) the educational structures that serve Latine students. The first article about Chicano and Puerto Rican colleges was published by legal scholar Michael Olivas (rest in power) in 1982, prior to the official recognition of HSIs in federal legislation. Olivas (1982) foreshadowed the *challenges and barriers* that HSIs would face, warning that without a historical or traditional mission to serve Chicanos and Puerto Ricans, these colleges would come to rely on only certain criteria for designation, including enrollment. Scholars have since noted that HSIs are unwilling to name themselves as HSIs in their mission statements despite the mission being a declaration of whom the organization serves (Andrade & Lundberg, 2018; Contreras et al., 2008; Malcom-Piqueux & Bensimon, 2015). In all his brilliance, Olivas laid out several core issues we would come to grapple with in HSI research and practice for years to come, including organizational identity, representation of faculty and administrators, and governance.

In 1995 Daniel Solórzano explored the baccalaureate origins of Chicana/o doctorates in the social sciences, which is arguably the first empirical article to name HSIs, with Solórzano citing a HACU annual report from 1991 for the HSI definition. Solórzano found that 7 of the top 10 producers of Chicana/o undergraduates who would go on to earn a doctorate were HSIs. Five years later Wolf-Wendel et al. (2000) found similar results, noting that HSIs were efficient producers of Black and Latina women graduates who would enter doctoral programs. These were early contributions to the HSI literature base showing the *significance of HSIs* for both Latine students and other students of color.

In summer 1998 a special issue of *New Directions for Higher Education* focused on MSIs, with three articles mentioning HSIs. O'Brien and Zudak (1998) noted that in 1994 Historically Black Colleges and Universities (HBCUs), Tribal Colleges, and HSIs represented less than one-third of all colleges in the United States, yet they enrolled over two-thirds of all students of color. They also stated that although HSIs were the newest MSI type, there were already 125 eligible HSIs enrolling 42% of all Latines, making them the largest of the three types. The authors' underlying argument was about the *increasing significance* of HSIs with regard to enrollment of Latine students. In the same special issue, Puerto Rican educator and policy expert Margarita Benítez provided a profile of HSIs and described the growth of the Hispanic and HSI population in the United States (1998). She also elevated Puerto Rican HSIs, describing their progress in enrollment as a result of federal financial aid and suggesting that, since all institutions in Puerto Rico were HSIs (n = 50), the overall number of HSIs (n = 131) was overinflated at that time (Benítez, 1998).

Berta Vigil Laden (rest in power) was also an early advocate of HSIs, publishing a series of articles about their significance (Hagedorn, 2007). In the early 2000s she provided a reflective history of HSIs, noting the factors that contributed to their creation, such as the 1960s Civil Rights Movement, the increase in Hispanic immigration, and the evolution of HACU as an important advocate (Laden, 2001). These descriptive articles became foundational to our understanding, *providing a definition and historical overview* of HSIs as a federal construct.

In 2004 Birtha Vigil Laden served as guest editor for a special issue of *Community College Journal of Research and Practice* that explored two-year HSIs (Laden, 2004a, 2004b). The special issue included seven articles about Latino issues in community colleges, with the authors describing a number of challenges affecting the Latine population, many of which would become germane to the HSI conversation. The authors also described the *educational structures that serve*

Latine students. For example, Hagedorn and Cepeda (2004) identified programs for Latine students available within several Hispanic-serving community colleges, including the Society of Hispanic Professional Engineers (SHPE) and the Puente Project. Other scholars would go on to argue that these programs and others, such as Educational Opportunity Program (EOP) and Chicana/o Studies, were the sole providers of servingness at HSIs (Garcia & Okhidoi, 2015).

A final dimension of the research in this era described the *contextual effects of HSIs*. For example, Muñoz (2009) found that "Latinas appeared to have greater access to leadership opportunities at Hispanic Serving Institutions (HSIs)," although she did not explore the contextual reasons (i.e., what is it about the HSI context that contributes to this finding?) (p. 172). Perna et al. (2010) showed significant findings about equity in enrollment and graduation as well as employment of full-time faculty and administrators in HSIs. In comparing predominantly white institutions (PWIs) to HSIs, they revealed there was equity in enrollment of Latine students at HSIs compared to non-HSIs, as well as equity in degree completion at both HSIs and PWIs that were public institutions. They also showed great inequities in the number of Latine-identified full-time faculty and administrators at all institutional types, even HSIs. Perna et al. (2010) helped to build the argument about the contextual effects of HSIs (i.e., the potential to advance equitable graduation rates) while posing some of the enormous challenges (i.e., low representation of Latine faculty and administrators).

The HSI scholarship burgeoned during the enrollment era, laying a foundation for what it means to be an HSI as defined by enrollment, eligibility, and grants. During the 26 years of the enrollment era, 168 articles were published that named HSIs as the context of the study, although most (n = 99) did not analyze or make sense of the HSI context in the article. A majority simply named the research site as an HSI but did not talk about what that meant to the campus or the study. Excelencia in Education also distributed a series of policy briefs about HSIs and several scholars coedited the first three books focused solely on HSIs: *Teaching Writing with Latino/a Students: Lessons Learned at*

Hispanic-Serving Institutions (Kirklighter et al., 2007), *Hispanic-Serving Institutions: Advancing Research and Transformative Practice* (Núñez et al., 2015), and *Hispanic-Serving Institutions in American Higher Education: Their Origin, and Present and Future Challenges* (Perez Mendez et al., 2015). These scholarly contributions laid the foundation for the transitional era.

Transitional Era Knowledge Production

HSI knowledge production during the transitional era (2019–) has steadily increased, with scholars advancing a more complex understanding of what it means to be an HSI beyond enrollment, eligibility, and grants. The research in this era draws on more critical perspectives for understanding HSIs, arguing that social justice, racial equity, educational liberation, humanizing environments, and community cultural wealth are foundational to serving. In 2019 my colleagues and I proposed the Multidimensional Conceptual Framework for Understanding Servingness at HSIs ("the servingness framework") based on a deep reflection on how scholars made sense of HSIs in their writing from 1992 to 2017 (Garcia et al., 2019a). We pulled together disparate ideas generated from journal articles and book chapters published during the enrollment era to propose a comprehensive framework for understanding what it means to truly serve Latine students.

The servingness framework deemphasizes enrollment, eligibility, and grants, and proposes a tangible way for HSIs to operationalize the *S* in HSIs. It includes "structures for serving" (e.g., curriculum, support services, faculty diversity, strategic plans, HSI grants) and academic and nonacademic "indicators of serving" (e.g., graduation rates, transfer rates, STEM degrees awarded, job placement, critical consciousness, racial-ethnic-Indigenous identity development, community engagement). Our core argument was that HSIs must change the way they serve Latine students by focusing on structural transformation, and they must measure servingness in more ways than one. In other words, equitable graduation rates are important, but not the sole indicator of serving Latine students well. The servingness framework stresses that enrollment, eligibility, and grants are simply insufficient for becoming socially just, equity-minded, antiracist HSIs.

A special issue of the *Association of Mexican American Educators (AMAE) Journal* published in late 2017 focused on HSIs, providing a foundation for the critical scholarship that would emerge during the transitional era. Cuellar et al. (2017) used critical race theory and community cultural wealth to challenge dominant notions of acceptable outcomes for college students as guided by Alexander Astin's Inputs-Environments-Outcomes (IEO) model. They argued that HSIs should empower students, and they proposed a series of empowerment outcomes, including positive academic self-concept, racial-ethnic identity, social justice orientation, graduate school aspirations, and navigational skills. Doran and Medina (2017) used historical methods to document the emergence of two HSIs in two different states. Of importance, they challenged the prevailing notion that HSIs accidentally become HSIs and instead showed that some campuses engaged in intentional efforts to increase access for Latine students, thus becoming "intentional HSIs." They also provided an alternative narrative about how some HSIs emerged because of the efforts of student activists on campus demanding increased access for Latines and the establishment of Latine programs, labeling these "grassroots HSIs."

In the same issue, Marin and Pereschica (2017) brought graduate student voices into the literature with participants stating they wanted to be included in the campus HSI efforts. This elevated the idea that multiple constituents should be included in the HSI movement on campus despite the fact that eligible HSIs are only defined by enrollment of undergraduate students. Similarly, Contreras (2017) provided a detailed analysis of faculty composition at two state systems in California—the California Community College and California State University. She showed the extreme disparities in the number of Latine students enrolled in each system compared to Latine faculty, amplifying the same issue that Perna et al. (2010) presented seven years earlier. Vargas et al. (2019) offered similar data, bringing in ratios of Latine-identified faculty to Latine-identified students at HSIs that had received Title V grants. On average the ratio was 1:146, showing the burden placed on the few Latine-identified faculty in HSIs.

In 2021 my HSI side sister Dra. Marcela Cuellar and I served as guest editors for a special topic collection of *AERA Open*. We called for articles that would advance an understanding of "intersectional servingness," conceptualized as an approach to serving Latine students in HSIs that accounts for "intersecting individual identities while simultaneously accounting for domains of power and historicity" (Garcia & Cuellar, 2023, p. 3). What we found was that the eight contributing authors or teams of authors used critical theories and critical research methods to "interrogate organizational, representational, intersubjective, and experiential domains of power and macrolevel, interlocking forces that evolve over time" (Garcia & Cuellar, 2023, p. 3). In each article, authors extended the servingness framework to challenge systems of oppression such as racism, anti-Blackness, patriarchy, coloniality of power, and nationalism, calling to question the ways HSIs perpetuate these systems while purporting to serve Latine students. In many ways, these sets of articles expressed the true essence of servingness in the transitional era, with researchers and practitioners pushing for more complex, more intersectional approaches to educating Latine students.

More than 160 journal articles about HSIs have already been published in the transitional era, some of which are guided by the servingness framework and other critical perspectives such as the decolonizing HSIs framework (Garcia, 2018). Of importance, authors in the transitional era began to complicate the *H* in HSIs, talking about queer Latines, mixed race Latines, and Indigenous Latines in HSIs (e.g., Cataño & González, 2021; Cristobal et al., 2021; González & Cataño, 2020; Kovats Sánchez, 2021). These authors (and others) challenged the reification of the term "Hispanic," pushing for a more intersectional approach to servingness. Scholars during this era also analyzed the HSI context from the perspective of Black, Indigenous, and Asian American students, faculty, and staff, providing a picture of HSIs as toxic and harmful to non-Latine people of color (e.g., Abrica et al., 2020; Comeaux et al., 2021; Desai & Abeita, 2017; Pirtle et al., 2021; Venegas et al., 2021; Zaragoza & Garcia, 2023).

We also saw the emergence of research that complicated the structures for serving at HSIs, with authors focusing on murals, art, sculptures, and door decorations as servingness (Garcia & Zaragoza, 2020; Meza, 2023), faculty and institutional governance as servingness (Garcia & Morgan, 2025; Villarreal Sosa et al., 2023), and family orientations as servingness (Covarrubias et al, 2020). The transitional era also gifted us with HSI books that have become mandatory reading for the changemakers in the movement: *Becoming Hispanic-Serving Institutions: Opportunities for Colleges and Universities* (Garcia, 2019), *Bordered Writers: Latinx Identities and Literacy Practices at Hispanic-Serving Institutions* (Baca et al., 2019), *Hispanic Serving Institutions (HSIs) in Practice: Defining "Servingness" at HSIs* (Garcia, 2020), and *Transforming Hispanic-Serving Institutions for Equity & Justice* (Garcia, 2023). We will continue to see critical HSI research emerge during this era, with this book being another offering to the HSI community.

Welcome to the HSI Movement—El Movimiento HSI

If you are new to the HSI movement, welcome y bienvenides! This introduction was intended to give you some HSI history, including HSI as a legislative construct and a scholarly exercise. Undeniably, the HEA legislation that legitimized HSIs and Title V and III grants are essential to the movement yet insignificant for creating deep-seated structural and cultural change. I argue that we have entered "the transitional era" of HSIs; meaning, a critical mass of eligible HSIs, eHSIs, and sHSIs are now focused on second-order change processes that will move us beyond enrollment, eligibility, and grant seeking and getting. Moreover, I argue that HSI scholarship is fueling the move toward transformation, with research and knowledge driving the emergence of HSI-minded practitioners at HSIs. Becoming HSI-minded is vital to the movement because a shift in the way people think about serving students will outlive the federal designation and grants. In chapter 1, I lay out the theoretical and methodological foundations of this book, highlighting what we know about how institutions of higher education change. The stories that follow in each chapter are about how people—grassroots leaders, changemakers, and organizers—are essential to change, and movement-based tactics are most effective, while the levers, practices, and policies of change also matter.

1

Organizational (Identity) Change

THE HSI MOVEMENT is about how HSIs can change, are changing, and should change in order to actualize a Latine-serving identity—and about the people driving the change. There are many ways to approach organizational change, but I frame it within the context of organizational identities. I have consistently argued that embracing an HSI organizational identity is vital, as an organizational identity represents the most central, distinct, and enduring aspects of the organization (Albert & Whetten, 1985; Garcia, 2017a, 2017b, 2019; Garcia et al., 2019b). Drawing on institutional theory and theories about organizational culture, I proposed a Typology of HSI Organizational Identities that included four types: Latine-enrolling, Latine-producing, Latine-enhancing, and Latine-serving (Garcia, 2017a). At the time of data collection in 2012, the data did not suggest movement between these identities, or what I call "organizational identity development" (Garcia et al., 2025). Making meaning of an HSI organizational identity was quite new, and the participants in my study struggled with this. In fact, the interview protocol that guided the study allowed them to imagine what it *could* mean to be Hispanic-serving. We co-constructed an ideal HSI identity together based on legitimizing forces of the field and proposed unique dimensions of an HSI, envisioning something not yet solidified in research or practice.

In 2015 my graduate students and I expanded the study from a single-site case study, which allowed me to develop theory and test hypotheses, to a multiple-site case study, which lent itself to replication and verification (Garcia et al., 2019b). Asking nearly identical questions and observing the same phenomena at three sites allowed me to experiment with the proposed concepts. I wrote about the three cases in the book *Becoming Hispanic-Serving Institutions: Opportunities for Colleges and Universities* and further theorized two of the four types, proposing the Model of a Latinx Enhancing Organizational Identity (Latine-enhancing identity) (Garcia, 2019, p. 70) and the Model of an Organizational Third Space (Latine-serving identity) (Garcia, 2019, p. 93). But I did not talk about movement through the four HSI identity types. Similar to the first study, the data did not suggest movement through identities. Otherwise stated, significant change was not happening.

I collected data again in 2022 in an attempt to observe movement between identity types. What emerged through data analysis is what I am calling "processes of change" or "servingness processes," which I describe in chapter 3. These are the processes that may lead a campus to move from one type to another—let's say Latine-enhancing to Latine-serving, or Latine-enrolling to Latine-producing. Processes are a series of tasks and activities that help the organization achieve its goals—in this case, to become Latine-serving. Other things that emerged in the data were the levers of change, or the instruments that support and enable the processes of change, which I describe in chapter 2. More specifically, HSI grants are essential levers of change that provide HSIs with the opportunity to pilot new programs and be innovative in their approach to servingness. Notably, a series of barriers to change also arose in the data, quite loudly, making them hard to ignore. Some of these barriers are described in chapter 5. These findings align with the influences on organizational identity development proposed by my coauthors and I, as we argue that both internal processes of change and external isomorphic influences have a strong effect on the socially constructed HSI identity and projected HSI image (Garcia et al., 2025).

With each study, I have contributed to a more nuanced understanding of HSI identity, yet movement between identities has remained elusive. But why? The simple answer is that organizational change and actualizing a Latine-serving identity take time, and I have not yet come in contact with an HSI that has a central, distinct, and enduring HSI identity. In other words, enrolling, eligible, and grant-seeking HSIs have not become unapologetic HSIs—to be an unapologetic HSI means to exist as an HSI without fear of being questioned or challenged, to confidently live out an HSI purpose, to embrace an HSI organizational identity without excluding others, and to wear your HSI-ness proudly (Garcia, 2024, September 9). HSIs are not there yet, but we have entered the transitional era, and change is happening. Although I may not ever write about an actualized Latine-serving identity, someone who is reading this book will, and that brings me great joy.

Dimensions of Identity

The Typology of HSI Organizational Identities includes two dimensions to help campuses operationalize an HSI identity: outcomes and organizational culture. I argued that colleges and universities create their identities by comparing themselves to similar organizations and drawing on the legitimized ways that organizations in an established field act (Pedersen & Dobbin, 2006; Whetten & Mackey, 2022). In the field of higher education, some of the most legitimized outcomes are graduation, labor market outcomes, and economic mobility. As such, HSI scholars and practitioners have consistently argued that HSIs must produce equitable academic outcomes for Latine students, including transfer, graduation, postbaccalaureate enrollment, STEM outcomes, and job placement. A focus on student outcomes is essential to embracing an HSI identity, which is where equity-minded leadership, campus equity plans, and the Seal of Excelencia come into the HSI organizational change process.

The flip side of the organizational identity coin is that organizations strive for uniqueness, with colleges and universities distinguishing themselves from similar institutions (Pedersen & Dobbin, 2006). There are many things that can make an HSI unique—a Latine-centered curriculum (not just in ethnic studies but across the entire curriculum, even in STEM and career technical programs); an equitable representation of Latine faculty, administrators, and trustees; opportunities to hear, speak, engage, and learn in Spanish (including bilingual or fully Spanish courses); Latine foods available on campus all the time (not just during special events); and public art or murals on campus that represent the collective identity and historical struggle of Latines. These are a few examples, but there are others being defined in real time, many of which we talk about on the podcast *¿Qué pasa, HSIs?* We have operationalized these unique dimensions as the "structures for serving," or the tangible ways that an HSI can assess the campus environment for ways it serves Latine students (Garcia et al, 2019a). A focus on the structures for serving is as important as the pursuit of equitable outcomes for Latine students, which is where HSI organizational change frameworks, including the servingness framework (Garcia et al, 2019a) and the transforming HSIs framework (Garcia, 2023), come into the HSI organizational change process.

The goal of transforming the educational structures is to make servingness a core part of the organizational culture. Culture, or the embedded assumptions, beliefs, and values, creates the context where organizational identity is established and maintained (Hatch & Schultz, 2002). In other words, creating a Latine-serving culture is essential to embodying a Latine-serving identity. Tierney (1988) gave us a framework to operationalize culture within postsecondary institutions inclusive of the environment, mission, socialization, information, strategy, and leadership, with many of these dimensions aligning with the HSI organizational change frameworks (i.e., servingness framework, transforming HSIs framework). Put another way, existing HSI organizational change frameworks are cultural frameworks.

Culture is also connected to change efforts, with Tierney (1988) arguing that administrators must understand the culture of their institutions in order to make decisions, address conflict, find solutions to problems, and lead change efforts. Kezar and Eckel (2002b) further posited that the culture affects change initiatives and that major shifts can impact the underlying belief system of the organization. As such, many have studied how organizational culture affects change efforts within colleges and universities. Miller and Holliday-Millard (2021) found that the organizational culture affected the adoption of a social justice course requirement at a Southern Christian liberal arts college. The environment and mission allowed faculty and students alike to merely "check the box" to fulfill the diversity requirement without making substantial change, while the culture of leadership allowed for informal decision-making that led to loose requirements for change.

Orphan and Hartley (2021) discovered that change is an ongoing process, which contradicts prevailing change theory suggesting the final stage of institutionalization occurs when the change becomes part of the organization's prevailing norms, behaviors, values, and culture. While continuous efforts to engage the culture was essential to change on the campuses they studied, a cultural shift was not the final destination. Nuñez (2024) argued that institutional logics, which like culture include the embedded assumptions and sensemaking frames used to make decisions within organizations, should look different within HSIs. She studied institutional logics within computer science departments at four HSIs that have a long-term commitment to servingness and found they had disrupted dominant institutional logics of prestige seeking and instead focused on access, talent development, and cultural responsiveness.

Both Outcomes and Culture

HSIs in transition must tend to both the student outcomes and the organizational culture as they manage their change efforts. I have argued that outcomes should be expansive and include both academic and liberatory outcomes (Garcia, 2023). Striving for equitable, legitimized outcomes such as graduation rates, transfer rates, labor market outcomes, and economic mobility is fundamental but not sufficient to achieving a unique HSI identity because all colleges and universities in the United States strive for those outcomes. HSIs must actively create a unique, culturally enhancing, antiracist, socially just environment that will enable liberatory outcomes and experiences. Liberation theory necessitates that we provide educational experiences, both in and out of the classroom, that allow students to develop their minoritized identity and an understanding of self with regard to their sociopolitical positioning in the world (Freire, 2014). Liberatory pedagogies compel us to provide educational opportunities for students to develop conscientization, or a critical consciousness, that evokes a desire to change the world (Freire, 2014). Liberatory praxis requires that students disrupt their colonizing mindsets taught in US educational systems, grapple with critical theory, and engage in action to disrupt the status quo (hooks, 1994).

In order to achieve liberatory outcomes and experiences for students in HSIs, we must tend to the organizational culture, the institutional logics, and the overall sensemaking efforts that drive organizational behavior. There must be a commitment to disrupting dominant culture and legitimizing logics that will enable an embodied Latine-serving identity. And yes, this will require us to navigate colonized institutional logics and legitimizing state and federal legislative structures that may help or hinder us in our work. We will need grassroots leaders and change agents to helm these efforts and administrators and positional leaders who will support the grassroots movement while managing change efforts and ensuring the economic and human resources are available to support the change. Overall, HSIs in transition must focus on shifting the organizational structures, culture, and logics for serving Latine students while simultaneously advancing equitable academic and liberatory experiences and outcomes. The change I am talking about is long-term, second-order, deep-seated change. It is going to take time, and we must be patient. But we must also engage in learning about how colleges change and specifically about how HSIs are changing.

How Colleges Change

There are decades of research about organizational change that can enhance our understanding of change management within an HSI context. Adrianna Kezar is a notable higher education scholar who has written extensively about how colleges and universities change. In the book *How Colleges Change: Understanding, Leading, and Enacting Change*, she provides a Multifaceted Framework for Understanding Change that is grounded in extensive research (Kezar, 2018). The framework includes four main dimensions: (1) type of change, (2) context for change, (3) agency/leadership, and (4) approach to change. Rather than describing the framework in detail, I will draw on aspects of the framework that are most relevant to HSI organizational (identity) change efforts.

The type of change HSIs must undertake is substantial, with HSI organizational change frameworks (i.e., servingness framework, transforming HSIs framework) providing a tangible outline of the efforts needed to become Latine-serving. I argue that everything from the mission and vision statements to the governance processes must be transformed, and call on all constituents to be a part of the process, including students, faculty, staff, administrators, trustees, alumni, families, community members, and external partners (Garcia, 2023; Garcia et al., 2019a). The scope of change is second order, "where the underlying values, assumptions, structures, processes, and culture [need] to be addressed in order for change to occur" (Kezar, 2018, p. 71). In other words, people within HSIs must fundamentally change their mindsets and engage in efforts to increase their HSI-mindedness.

Arguably, HSIs have only focused on first-order changes during the enrollment era, which are minor improvements and adjustments. These first-order changes are facilitated by grants, with many HSIs creating tutoring programs for Latine STEM students, mentoring programs for first-generation Latine students, summer bridge programs for low-income Latine students, or Title V centers where students can access all of the above. The problem with these first-order change efforts is that the fundamental values and the culture of the organization are unchanged. In fact, these first-order changes may actually reinforce the misconception that special programs are sufficient to adequately serve Latine college students. Although wraparound programs may work for some, many Latine students do not access these support structures, leaving them underserved or unserved altogether. Instead, HSIs must engage in second-order change processes that go beyond grant-funded programmatic efforts. Kezar (2018) suggests that even some of the efforts happening in the transitional era, such as HSI task forces, HSI strategic plans, and faculty training and development, are first-order changes. These efforts may help campuses assess the scope of change needed, but additional work is needed to change the entire campus's mindset for serving Latine students.

There are also different levels of change, including individual, group, organizational, and sectoral, according to Kezar (2018). In the same work, Kezar contends we must assess each level to determine what changes are needed to achieve our ultimate outcome. At the individual level, folks must become HSI-minded, actively learning what it means to be an HSI beyond enrollment, eligibility, and grant seeking and getting, and studying the best practices and extensive research on supporting and educating Latine college students. This includes all members of the organization, including presidents, vice presidents, trustees, and external partners (Garcia, 2023). At the group level, departments must become HSI-minded too, engaging in practices that consider and center the history and community cultural wealth of Latine students. The group level may also include the discipline with active efforts to educate colleagues in the field on the unique ways we educate Latine students and do research with and for Latine people. The group level is where conversations about the rewards structure may also happen. For example, do promotion and tenure processes assess individual efforts to serve Latine students?

I have argued consistently that change must happen at the organizational level, providing HSI frameworks to help HSIs identify the structural and policy shifts that must occur. The enterprise level is the field level, which includes the over 600 eligible HSIs and the additional emerging and striving institutions as well as the associations and partners shaping the HSI narrative. Arguably, we need second-order change at every level in order to become Latine-serving institutions.

Overall, Kezar (2018) argues that second-order change is difficult for colleges and universities because they have a long-standing, enduring mission that is in tension with the Latine-serving identity I advocate for. It leaves me wondering whether attaining a Latine-serving identity is really possible. Whether the change is called "transformational," "punctuated," or "double-loop learning," it is "so substantial that it alters the operating systems, underlying values, and culture of an organization or system" (Kezar, 2018, p. 85). Kezar also maintains that structural changes are necessary but not enough, and that attitudinal or cultural evidence of a shift must be present—a change in group interactions, a change in language used, a change in relationships with external partners, and so on. She offers two organizational perspectives—sensemaking and organizational learning. Both are similar in that they advocate for a shift in underlying assumptions and values, although organizational learning requires a more data-driven approach (Kezar, 2018). Arguably, the Seal of Excelencia is an organizational learning approach designed for HSIs that calls on campus constituents to dive into multiple years of disaggregated student-level data to identify issues and opportunities to better serve Latines, yet it doesn't require the sensegiving activities that may lead to long-term cultural change.

Kezar (2018) offers a series of sensegiving activities that are helpful to advance change efforts, many of which are taking place on HSI campuses in the transitional era: ongoing and widespread campus conversations about the change (I am invited to many HSI campuses to start or engage in servingness conversations), collaborative leadership (I see faculty, staff, administrators, and increasingly more students engaging in HSI work), developing cross-departmental teams and working groups (the HSI task force is often cross-departmental), sponsoring faculty and staff development opportunities (ESCALA and AHSIE are leading the way in this realm), drawing on and discussing external ideas (this is the goal of the podcast *¿Qué pasa, HSIs?*), flexible vision (the HSI vision evolves as more people join the HSI movement), creating documents and concept papers (many campuses create an internal HSI report to guide their work), and preparing and giving public lectures (campuses and regional consortia are hosting webinars, visioning sessions, and public lectures with local and national scholar practitioners).

Understanding the type of change needed to shift a campus from a Latine-enrolling identity to a Latine-serving identity is important, yet Kezar (2018) includes other considerations in her change framework. She stresses that campuses must understand the context for change, including the social, political, and economic factors, external stakeholders, and the higher-education sector. The political climate under the 47th president of the United States, for example, has haunted the HSI community as Title V grants were defunded, and grant directors and grant teams lost their jobs. The trauma of this experience has had profound effects on many HSIs and could hinder change over time. Kezar (2018) also includes leadership and agency of change as dimensions of the change framework, which are directly translated to the transforming HSIs framework, with her laying out three leadership approaches for organizations to consider: top-down versus bottom-up (grassroots) leadership, collective leadership, and shared leadership. A collective grassroots leadership approach is common in HSIs, with staff and faculty leading from the margins, yet we are seeing more high-level administrators get involved in HSI efforts too.

In assessing the type of change needed, the context for change, and the most appropriate leadership tactics to use, Kezar (2018) stresses change agents must carefully pick an approach to change that makes the most sense. Common approaches are scientific management, evolutionary, political, social cognition, cultural, and institutional, although she notes that a multitheory approach has the best chance of working. In drawing on multiple theories, change agents can develop strategies and tactics for managing change. As noted, I drew heavily on cultural and institutional theories to develop the Typology of HSI Organizational Identities. I used institutional theory because the emergence of HSIs originates from the external environment, with the most distinct features being the changing demographics of college-going students (specifically Latine-identified students) and the federal legislation that created the HSI construct (specifically the reauthorization of HEA). While some campuses created specific policies to increase enrollment of Latine students (intentional HSIs) and others opened their doors as a result of student demands for increased access (grassroots HSIs), many HSIs emerged because of the changing demographics of the surrounding community with no real effort to engage with the Latine community (accidental HSIs) (Doran & Medina, 2017).

Even those intentionally striving to become HSIs (sHSIs) are affected by the external environment. The type of change is thus unplanned for many HSIs, which is a key characteristic of environmental theory. I continue to think cultural theory is most relevant to the type of change that needs to happen within HSIs, as cultural theory calls for second-order change and a paradigmatic shift. The process of change tends to be long and nonlinear, and it happens at multiple levels of the organization, which is what I am observing in HSIs as they transition. A third theory relevant to HSIs in transition is the political approach, which is often used when the change causes a dialectical tension of values and norms. A key element of the political theory is social movement, and the tactics include coalition building, ally development, negotiation, and collective visioning. In the next section, I turn to a specific political theory I think HSIs in transition could benefit from: emergent strategy.

Emergent Strategy

Emergent strategy (brown, 2017) changed my scholarly life. It was the theory I was looking for to make sense of organizational change through a critical, movement-based approach. Since writing my dissertation in 2013, I have believed that organizational change was the framework I needed to make sense of HSIs in transition. But I wasn't ready to talk about organizational change back then, because it wasn't happening during the enrollment era. Moreover, the organizational change frameworks I found in higher education and organizational behavior literature were not aligning with my vision for transformation. Emergent strategy was the framework I didn't know I needed, but the Universe knew, and so emergent strategy came to me. I have since become a huge fan of adrienne maree brown, who wrote the book *Emergent Strategy: Shaping Change, Changing Worlds*. Other authors have embraced her teachings and brought emergent strategy to life for me. I have consumed their writings and pay homage to the Black, queer, trans, and immigrant femmes who gave me a social movement framework to make sense of organizational change for HSIs. Ritchie (2023) says we don't need to convince the entire organization to be on board with the change we envision; we just need kindred spirits that are willing to do the work. And there are many kindred spirits in the HSI movement.

Emergent strategy is a justice-centered, visionary, collaborative approach to envisioning and enacting change. Emergent strategy is "for people who want to radically change the world" (brown, 2017, p. 4). Grounded in her work as an activist and organizer and drawing inspiration from science fiction, specifically the work of Octavia Butler, brown provides a framework for creating new futures together. She argues that dreaming of new futures is a core part of justice work, which aligns closely with my own freedom dreaming with and for HSIs (Garcia, 2023) and feels appropriate to use as a way to make sense of organizational change in HSIs. In addition to dreaming of new futures, emergent strategy provides a set of practices and processes for change; it moves us from envisioning to doing. Emergent strategy provides an abundance of possibilities for imagining a world free of oppressive, carceral practices while creating safe communities where people can thrive (Ritchie, 2023).

Emergent strategy has six elements. The first is *fractals*, or the relationship between small and large, which includes the self (small) and the organization (large). In creating new futures together, large-scale change emerges from small-scale action. Other things to consider as part of fractals is that organizational change relies on a network of people and resources. Or as stated by brown (2017), "Every member of the community holds pieces of the solution, even if we are all engaged in different layers of the work" (p. 63). Another thing to consider is that emergent strategy does not call for top-down approaches and linear planning but rather collective networking and action from the bottom. Ritchie (2023) states, "Emergent strategies invite us to act based on shared values and principles at a smaller scale, and to connect our actions across time and space into networks with the power to shape complex systems" (p. 10). The framework does not necessarily require state-based reforms or the acquisition of state power in order to implement these changes; it requires small communities focused on networking, relationship building, sharing resources, and decision-making (Ritchie, 2023). Emergent strategy honors small-scale, intentional, collaborative change, and much of the HSI work is small scale.

The second element is *intentional adaptation*, which is the way people, organizations, and systems change. Adaptation is about the individual person, plant, or animal changing itself to better fit into a new situation, environment, or organization. Emergent strategy expects and embraces change as inevitable but plans for it in intentional ways to remain relevant. For HSIs, the change in student demographics is inevitable and expected, yet the organization must adapt to the identities, needs, and lived experiences of Latine students. Intentional adaptation is informed by vision, with the intent to move toward growth and regeneration. Yet Ritchie (2023) reminds us that emergent strategy requires collective action too, not just collective intention. The collective intention emerges from the small group of individuals driving change, not from the upper echelons of society. Ritchie (2023) states that emergent strategy is grounded in Indigenous ways of knowing, with collectivist approaches driving the intentional adaptation guided by planned strategies and detailed blueprints for implementation, while remaining flexible.

Interdependence and decentralization are combined to make up the third element of emergent strategy, which brown (2017) summarizes as "who we are and how we share" (p. 83). Change is facilitated by the authentic connections we have with others, with relationships driving change. Emergent strategy accepts decentralization and independence among individuals, groups, and organizations but requires relationships and common connections to drive the change collectively. Ritchie (2023) also stresses that change occurs through relationships, small networks, and communities of practice. These networks share resources and information and build critical connections, which is how we impact larger systems. brown (2017) also emphasizes that interdependence requires individuals to be seen, be wrong, and be willing to ask for help. These are important characteristics of leaders in the movement, as brown (2017) reminds us that there are no rock stars in the movement; we all make mistakes and need each other. The multitude of leaders in the movement shall be collaborative, accountable, and vulnerable.

The fourth element is called "*nonlinear and iterative.*" As noted by brown (2017), "Transformation does not happen in a linear way" (p. 105), an observation that is essential to emergent strategy. Change will occur in cycles, and failure is inevitable as part of the process. Instead of being discouraged by failure, we shall learn from our mistakes and ask ourselves how to continue moving forward after setbacks. Bringing people into movements, building collective consciousness, and enhancing our power to make change is a process, and it may ebb and flow. A nonlinear process allows for growth and learning—a feedback loop, so to speak, where experimentation, feedback, and criticism are welcomed. brown (2017) suggests that loss and mourning and grief may be a part of the nonlinear process, and letting go may be inevitable. As part of the iterative process, newcomers will join the movement, and others will leave it, and we need to welcome and embrace these changes. Normalizing change and learning from it is a part of emergent strategy.

Resilience, the fifth element, is the ability to recover, transform, become strong, and continue to be successful after adversity and trauma. Resilience is a core dimension of emergent strategy, seen as beautiful and powerful. When social justice actors experience trauma, resilience is necessary to keep going. It enables a focused and renewed energy for achieving the desired change. Resilience allows for the transformation of toxic energy and conflict into solutions and actions. There is also learning, with emergent strategy allowing us to learn as we seek to dismantle the complex systems we are a part of. It means we commit to action "aimed at dismantling inter-locking systems of oppression at every scale," even when faced with adversity and trauma (Ritchie, 2023, p. 31). Resilience enables strength and liberation despite setbacks experienced while fighting for change.

The final element is *creating more possibilities*, which is the process of continuing to change over time, rather than viewing change, or even transformation and justice, as an end goal. Freedom, abolition, and liberation are processes, not destinations. Instead, the goals and intentions continue to reinvent themselves within the movement. For HSIs, this means the goal of "becoming" an HSI or Latine-serving institution is never realized, as this identity will continue to adapt over time. Emergent strategies align with abolitionist futures and freedom dreaming, stressing that we must first envision a world we want to see in order to make it a reality. Emergent strategy is a vision of how change can happen, how we can rebuild and design new systems. Ritchie (2023) states, "Emergent strategies point us toward the necessity of creating luscious, generative spaces and practices that make room for visioning the world we want and inviting people into creating it with us, iteration and adaption to meet the needs of participants and of the moment, opportunities to learn from our mistakes and for fostering transformation and building resilience" (p. 27). Creating new possibilities is grounded in transformative justice, or the idea of "transform[ing] the root causes of injustices" (brown, 2017, p. 133). In many ways this brings together other elements of emergent strategy, as transformative justice requires the fractals, or individual parts, to work together in decentralized and interdependent ways to intentionally adapt with a goal toward justice, liberation, and healing.

For me, emergent strategy gives us hope in the HSI movement. It is not easy to change colleges and universities that have historically oppressed minoritized people, historically been exclusive, and historically harmed communities of color. And that is essentially the work grassroots leaders in HSIs are doing. Emergent strategy provides hope that we can change postsecondary institutions by organizing, collaborating, and building relationships. It reminds us that small changes are necessary and effective on the path toward large-scale changes. Although that can feel discouraging to the organizers in the HSI movement, incremental and intentional adaptation are the foundations of an emergent strategy approach. But so is freedom dreaming and envisioning new futures. We can't build the HSIs we hope for without imagining them first. In chapter 6, I envision a proud, unapologetic, Latine-serving HSI, based on the empirical data in *The HSI Movement* and guided by my own vision for what can and should be.

Methodological Approach of This Book

The HSI Movement is about HSIs in transition and uses a storytelling method, which has its roots in social sciences, humanities, and law (Solórzano & Yosso, 2001). Specifically, I use a counterstory method, with the goal to highlight societal inequities, challenge the dominant narratives in society, and call for social justice and action (Solórzano & Yosso, 2002). Counter-storytelling is a method that comes from ethnic studies, women and gender studies, Marxism and neo-Marxism, and critical legal studies as a way to center the experiential knowledge of people of color, challenge the dominant ideology, and commit to social justice (Solórzano & Yosso, 2001). Counter-storytelling also has its roots in longstanding qualitative traditions such as grounded theory and theoretical sensitivity, and it specifically uses Delgado Bernal's (1998) conceptualization of cultural intuition. Cultural intuition allows for data, theory, personal experiences, ancestral wisdom, and community knowledge to inform the analytic process.

The stories in this book are called "composite stories," which Solórzano and Yosso (2002) describe as drawing on multiple forms of data and using characters placed in social, historical, and political situations to illuminate subordination and forms of oppression. The counterstories in this book are grounded in empirical evidence I collected in one-on-one interviews in fall 2022, and they are illuminated by my own experiences as an HSI scholar who works with and trains the HSI community. I also drew from existing research and stories from my own podcast, *¿Qué pasa, HSIs?*, to further develop the counterstories. I use storytelling to show how practitioners are conceptualizing the organizational transformation process at HSIs from their unique positions within the institutions. Often their conceptualizing is marginalized, as many of the participants I talked to and regularly work with are not in formal leadership positions; instead, they work as grassroots leaders to change the institution.

Using counterstories allowed the data to emerge in more engaging ways than a typical display of data offers. The stories are grounded in empirical data and truth, but they are pseudofictional; meaning, they are imaginary and did not happen as described. The characters and institutions are also modified to protect the identities of the participants in the study. Although I often use direct quotes from participants, they are weaved together to tell a story, and that weaving includes fictional characters expressing the thoughts of multiple other characters. All characters but one are created in the image of real participants in the study. As a form of member checking and reciprocity, I sent individual chapters to eight participants who were used either as narrators or main characters. I asked them to review their chapter, affirm it was accurate, and make any edits needed to protect their identity. Six of the eight requested minor changes to their chapter, and all eight agreed to be highlighted as narrators or main characters. I am forever grateful for their stories and generosity.

Data Sources

The data came from a study about HSI organizational identities and how they change. The purpose of the study was to explore the organizational change process within the context of the organizational identities of HSIs. Data were collected from August 2022 to December 2022 with the goal of investigating how HSIs, emerging HSIs, and striving HSIs move from Latine-enrolling to Latine-serving identities. Specifically, I collected data to understand how college and university educators and decision-makers are transforming the educational structures to better serve Latine and low-income students within HSIs. I interviewed them individually by Zoom, asking them questions about their individual and campus HSI efforts. The interview protocol aligned with the Typology of HSI Organizational Identities (Garcia, 2017a), focusing on outcomes and culture/structures, yet the questions were more expansive and based on emerging HSI research. For example, in the original typology, the outcomes were limited to graduation, job placement, and graduate school aspirations, yet based on continuous research, I included liberatory outcomes in this study (Garcia, 2021, 2023). The structures have also been complicated through ongoing research (Garcia, 2023; Garcia et al., 2019a), allowing me to explore them more closely in this study.

I personally interviewed 32 educators and decision-makers at 29 unique HSIs in transition (2 participants worked at the same two-year HSI, and 3 participants worked at the same four-year HSI). A summary of the sample is found in table 1.1, with pseudonyms used to protect the identities of the participants. I collected the survey participants' demographic information through open-ended questions, with exact responses to the sex/gender and race/ethnicity questions seen in table 1.1 but aggregated here. By sex/gender, the sample includes 25 women and 7 men. By race/ethnicity, the sample includes 26 Latine and 6 other races/ethnicities (including mixed race). To maintain anonymity, exact position titles are not revealed and instead aggregated and described here. By position, there were 7 faculty, inclusive of assistant through full professors but exclusive of academic administrators; 19 staff, inclusive of all levels including coordinators, directors, and various other positions; and 6 administrators, inclusive of associate deans or higher and vice presidents or higher. Nine participants held HSI-specific positions at the time of the interview, such as HSI grant directors and project coordinators, as well as non-grant-funded positions like HSI director and director of Hispanic initiatives.

My former graduate student researcher Dra. Marialexia Zaragoza collected additional information about the campuses; she labeled the participants' campuses as two-year or four-year, HSIs, emerging HSIs, or striving HSIs, and identified whether they had acquired Title III and V grants. At the time of their interviews, participants worked at four-year universities (n = 20) and two-year colleges (n = 12) as well as 25 public and 7 private institutions across eight states. States are not revealed to help maintain anonymity of the participants. Two participants worked at striving HSIs, and 2 worked at emerging HSIs, while the rest were employed at eligible HSIs. More than half (n = 18) had at least one federal HSI grant (Title III or V) at the time of the interview, while 14 did not. Only 4 institutions had received the Seal of Excelencia.

All these data points were included in the analysis, allowing for the composite narratives to emerge. The aim of the study was to describe the organizational change process and the challenges faced by HSIs and the people within them. The stories elevate the voices of practitioners at HSIs and the ways they are transforming institutions.

Transitioning HSIs

The HSI Movement is for the freedom dreamers in HSIs, for the grassroots leaders and organizers who can envision a new future for HSIs, for the changemakers who believe in liberation and empowerment for minoritized students in colleges and universities. This book is a continuation of the freedom dream I offered in *Transforming Hispanic-Serving Institutions for Equity & Justice*—but the empirical data here bring the freedom dream to life. The counterstories represent the

Table 1.1
Study Participants

Name	Race/Ethnicity	Sex/Gender	Position	Campus
Anastasia	Black biracial	Female/cisgender	Admin	4-year HSI
Araceli	Latinx Mexican	Woman	Staff	2-year HSI
Billy	Hispanic	Male	Admin	4-year HSI
Cesar	White	Female	Staff	4-year HSI
Connie	Mexican American	Female	Admin	2-year HSI
Daniel	Latino Mexican American	Male	Staff	2-year HSI
Don Francisco	Latino Mexican American	Male	Faculty	4-year HSI
Dra. Zapata	Latina	Female	Admin	2-year HSI
Eli	Hispanic/Latina	Female	Staff	4-year eHSI
Elizabeth	Latina	Female	Staff	4-year HSI
Esperanza	Chicana	Female	Staff	4-year HSI
Estrellita	Mexican	Female	Staff	2-year HSI
Gudelia	Mexican American	Female	Faculty	4-year HSI
Libby	Hispanic/Latina/Chicana	Female/cisgender	Faculty	4-year HSI
Lily	White	Female	Staff	4-year sHSI
Lucia	White Mexican American	Female	Staff	4-year HSI
Margarita	Chicana	Female	Staff	4-year HSI
Maria	White/Hispanic/Native	Female	Faculty	2-year HSI
Maya	Indian	Female	Staff	4-year HSI
Michelle	Latina	Female	Staff	2-year HSI
Natasha	Latina	Female	Faculty	4-year eHSI
Oscar	Hispanic	Male	Staff	2-year HSI
Pablo	Puerto Rican	Male	Staff	2-year HSI
Paulina	Latina	Female	Staff	4-year HSI
Rosalía	Hispanic	Female	Faculty	4-year HSI
Señor Reyes	Puerto Rican	Male	Staff	4-year sHSI
Skyler	Latinx Central American	Man	Faculty	4-year HSI
Sophie	Mexican	Female	Staff	4-year HSI
Suzette	Latina/Chicana	Female	Admin	4-year HSI
Taylor	Multiracial	Female	Admin	2-year HSI
Vanessa	Latina Puerto Rican	F	Staff	2-year HSI
Victoria	Mexican American/Chicana	Female/woman	Staff	2-year HSI

Note: Participants indicated race/ethnicity and sex/gender through open-ended questions.

successes and struggles of HSI grassroots leaders who show up to do hard work every day. Changing an entire institution is hard, but there are strategies and tactics that can be used to become an unapologetic HSI. I use the narrators in each chapter to provide hope in the process of change, as seen in their stories of movement, struggle, and sometimes joy, and to map the data onto various dimensions of emergent strategy.

In chapter 2, our narrator, Victoria, helps us understand how grants can be leveraged to advance organizational change. The challenge for HSIs is to use grants to advance deep-seated, second-order change. Other characters join Victoria to reveal how focusing on the emergent strategy dimension *fractals* has the potential to move us from micro- to macrolevel change. In chapter 3, our narrator, Nayeli, returns (IYKYK) to highlight the processes of organizational change that are happening in HSIs. I call these "processes of servingness," which are tasks and activities that can help campuses move through HSI organizational change frameworks (i.e., the servingness framework and the transforming HSIs framework). These processes are also reflective of *intentional adaptation* in the emergent strategy framework. Chapter 4 is about grassroots leadership and narrated by Connie, who helps us understand what it means to lead from the middle. Chapter 4 conceptualizes the emergent strategies of *interdependence and decentralization*. In chapter 5, our narrators, Vanessa and Araceli, have a reflective conversation about the barriers to change in HSIs. These barriers make it hard for change agents to enact the HSI vision, with some barriers so substantial that people stop trying. Moreover, the barriers remind us that *resilience* is a necessary part of change, as noted in the emergent strategy framework. This chapter offers hope to the dreamers, the grassroots leaders, the changemakers, and the organizers in HSIs; you are not alone in the struggle, and you are on the right track. In chapter 6, I envision an unapologetic HSI, leaning into brown's (2017) call to *create more possibilities* for HSI futures. I encourage you, the reader, to keep dreaming, keep envisioning, and keep working for better colleges and universities for Latine students.

2

HSI Grants as Levers of Change

Every member of the community holds pieces of the solution, even if we are all engaged in different layers of the work.
—adrienne maree brown, *Emergent Strategy: Shaping Change, Changing Worlds* (2017)

THE HSI ENROLLMENT ERA WAS DEFINED by enrollment, eligibility, and grants, with the funding offered by the federal government by way of competitive grants being one of the most essential levers of change for HSIs, thus far. Funding and investments are capacity-building policy instruments that carry hopes for future returns (McDonnell & Elmore, 1987), with Title V, Part A and Part B, and Title III, Part F falling into this category. Competitive funding to eligible HSIs can be up to $600,000 a year for five years. Although it is highly competitive—nearly 70% of eligible HSIs apply and only 30% successfully receive Title V grants (Aguilar-Smith & Yun, 2023)—HSIs that acquire Title V and Title III grants may be in a unique position to positively influence the educational outcomes of Latine students. Research has shown HSIs that receive Title V grants have an increased percentage of bachelor's degrees awarded to Latine students (Perez, 2020). In the same study, Perez found that student services expenditures at HSIs are positively correlated with an increase in degrees awarded, with many HSIs using their Title V and Title III grants to enhance student services. In contrast, Piñeda (2010) found no significant effect on degree attainment for Latine students who attend HSIs that acquire Title V funding.

Despite these divergent findings, I have consistently claimed that graduation rates cannot be the sole indicator of servingness (Garcia, 2017a, 2019). My argument is based on the fact that graduation rates are determined by many factors, some of which are beyond institutional control (i.e., student characteristics such as income levels). Instead, I call on HSIs to acknowledge the variables we cannot control, accept students and all their community cultural wealth as they are, and focus on what we can do—transform our colleges and universities to better serve Latine students. I have stressed the need to focus on the structural ways we serve students through the curriculum, pedagogy, student support services, cultural centers, cocurricular offerings, and physical infrastructure, to name a few (Garcia, 2023). I also contend the processes we engage in, including, among others, the decisions we make, the policies we pass, the people we hire, the community organizations we work with, and the funders we accept money from are forms of servingness (Garcia, 2023). A burgeoning body of research shows that Title V and Title III grants have been used to transform campus infrastructures and processes, and in some cases campus culture and institutional logics, making them important levers of change for HSIs.

Some HSIs have focused on making substantial changes to the campus infrastructure with their Title V and Title III funding, including launching new programs and services for students. UC Santa Cruz (UCSC), a four-year Hispanic Serving Research Institution (HSRI), used Title V funding to host a regional family conference, which included bilingual English and Spanish workshop offerings for incoming students and their families about topics such as financial aid, transitioning to college, and destigmatizing asking for help (Covarrubias et al., 2020). The overall goal was to increase students' and families' sense of belonging on campus. Roberts and Lucas (2022) wrote about a dually designated HSI and AANAPISI in California that started a Title V center to support first-year Latine students with identified courses and peer mentoring. The center also offered counseling and psychological services, and it provided an overall sense of community and encouragement. Campuses have also used HSI funding to launch summer bridge programs for STEM students (Masters et al., 2020), peer mentoring programs for STEM students (Cruz et al., 2021), learning communities for transfer students (Kato & Marinez, 2020), and lecture series for increasing Latine aspirations for graduate school (López et al., 2020).

Other HSIs have used their funding to address the campus culture for servingness, with an emphasis on changing campus processes and individual mindsets rather than implementing programs. Springfield Technical Community College, a two-year HSI in Massachusetts, invested in faculty and staff professional development with their HSI grant funding, focusing on awareness building around inequities that Latine and low-income students face and best practices for serving them (Griffin-Fennell & Lerner, 2020). UCSC launched a multicultural advising conference for advisers across campus, including those in residential colleges, student success areas, and transfer centers, to help them learn how to holistically serve Latine and low-income students (Sánchez Ordaz et al., 2020). The conference included information about microaggressions and microaffirmations in an effort to change the culture of advising on campus.

Dominican University, a four-year Catholic HSI in Illinois, invested in STEM faculty development by sending them to ESCALA Educational Services' STEM mini course (Petrov & Garcia, 2021). They also used Title V funds to supplement the development of a Truth, Racial Healing, and Transformation Center that supports faculty and staff development as antiracist and social justice educators. Adams State University, a four-year HSI in Colorado, built a "15-year foundation of intentional equity work facilitated by Title V grants," which included a weeklong teaching institute that engaged 78 faculty and staff and the launching of eight curriculum innovation teams (Cramblet Alvarez et al., 2023, p. 1541). They also facilitated faculty and staff learning to become experts on high-impact practices that could support their curriculum redesign and eventually launched new curricula that acknowledges students' identities and the region's history.

Overall we know a majority of HSIs invest their Title V and Title III funds into the infrastructure (Boland, 2018; Santiago et al., 2016), and a growing body of research has documented the processes of change taking place (e.g., Cramblet Alvarez et al., 2023; Franco & Muñiz, 2022; Petrov & Garcia, 2021). In this chapter, I focus on grant implementation, arguing that HSI grants were essential levers of change prior to Title V, Part A and Part B being defunded on September 10, 2015. The grants allowed HSI leaders to use emergent strategies to practice at a small scale what they wanted to see at the campus level. But brown (2017) reminds us of what she learned from activist and author Grace Lee Boggs: that we must also transform ourselves in order to transform the world. The educators who led HSI grants were also fundamental to this work as they were often transforming themselves in order to transform the institution. Some had a greater vision for ways to transform the campus culture, institutional logics, and HSI mindsets, which is true transformation, but they were often working against the status quo of institutional life. Although discretionary HSI grants were defunded under the 47th presidential administration, in this chapter I argue that small-scale change can lead to deeper transformation, and the examples offered remain exemplars of change.

Understanding How HSI Grants Initiate Change

This counterstory is about how HSI grants were leveraged to create change. HSI grants had the potential to be key structures for serving as they allowed HSIs to pilot new programs for Latine students, train faculty and staff to be effective educators, fund new infrastructures on campus, and redesign curriculum to center Latine ways of knowing, to name a few initiatives (Garcia et al., 2019a). This counterstory takes place at a (fictional) meeting for Alianza de HSI Directors, a (fictional) organization that supports HSI directors across the US who either direct Title V or Title III grants or are the campus HSI director overseeing HSI activities, irrespective of HSI grants. The Alianza meets virtually throughout the year and hosts one in-person meeting annually. The two-day in-person meeting is hosted by an HSI community college in Colorado. The story is narrated by Victoria, a newly appointed (fictional) HSI director at a (fictional) HSI community college.

Alianza de HSI Directors Meeting

8:16 a.m. The meeting starts at 9:00 a.m. in one of the hotel's meeting rooms. I have time to grab a coffee downstairs before we get started. This is my first meeting as the newly appointed campus HSI director at El Sol Community College, and the meeting organizers have asked me to present what we've been working on. I'm nervous but throw on my hoop "doctora" earrings that give me the poderosa energy I need. I sneak one last look in the hotel-room mirror and take a selfie to capture my flower dress, orange blazer, and platform Mary Janes before heading to the lobby.

9:00 a.m. We gather in the meeting room, where we all search for chairs at the round tables. Our virtual meetings are typically small, but this in-person meeting is larger, probably 40 or 50 people trying to find a seat. Now I'm really nervous. I find a seat, place my bag on the chair and notebook on the table, and head to the breakfast table at the side of the room to get a concha and more coffee.

The meeting organizer quiets us down and begins. "Bienvenides a todes, we are excited to have you join us for the annual Alianza de HSI Directors meeting. How many first-time attendees do we have?" A third of the participants raise their hands. "Qué bonito, let's clap it up for our first-time attendees." The crowd cheers with excitement. "My name is Benito, I use 'they' and 'them' pronouns, and I currently serve as cochair for Alianza. The goal of the meeting today is to network, share ideas, and support each other through challenges faced on campus as they pertain to our HSI work. Our servingness work is filled with peaks and valleys, wins and losses, two steps forward and three steps backward, and we are here for each other." Participants snap in agreement and nod their heads. Some have facial expressions that suggest they've had more losses than wins. "We will start the meeting with a mindfulness activity and then move into campus presentations. We will have two short presentations from campuses that are making significant progress in their paths toward servingness, with guided discussion following the presentations. Then we will have lunch. Any questions before we get started?"

9:12 a.m. I'm happy that we'll start with a mindfulness activity, as it will help settle my nerves before my presentation. I see on the agenda that I'm the second presenter, which also eases my mind. I don't know why I'm so nervous. These are my peers, my friends, mis compañeros. I can do this.

9:53 a.m. The first presenter prepares by pulling up their slides. I take advantage of the time to talk to my table neighbors. I meet Alejandra and Susana. Alejandra has been an HSI director for three years at an emerging HSI in Kansas. Susana is a Title V HSI director in New York. I share that I'm a new HSI director on my campus, a role that's funded by the president's office as a way to coordinate HSI efforts beyond the grant activities. We've been an HSI for over 20 years, and it took that long to get this level of commitment from the institution. We're excited that we're finally making it happen, even if it took a while to get here.

Synthesizing Multiple Grants to Build Momentum

Benito introduces the first speaker, Paulina, who is an HSI project coordinator at a four-year HSI. She greets the group. "Buenos días colegas. Gracias por permitirme hablarles esta mañana. My name is Paulina, and I use 'she,' 'her,' and 'ella' pronouns. I am here on behalf of our Title V project director, who was unable to make it. I've been in my role for 10 months. Prior to this role, I was a student on campus, and I worked with the HSI team for two years before pursuing my master's degree. After getting my master's degree, I applied for the Title V project coordinator position, and I got the job. Today I'm going to share some best practices and lessons learned from our HSI grant projects."

Paulina moves to her first slide, providing an overview of her campus's HSI efforts. "La Playa University has been HSI eligible for 10 years and has received five HSI grants, including Title III and Title V, Part A and Part B. With each grant, we have built on the previous, elevating various components. With the first couple of grants, we were working at the undergraduate level, like what is needed to make sure students are coming to campus and feeling comfortable and ready to tackle their academics, you know, academic aspects of being a university student, but also the first-generation challenges they experience. Then once they get to campus, making sure they're actually succeeding in their classes, including the gateway classes that we redesigned as part of our grant. But then we noticed other equity gaps at the university and that we were failing graduate students and transfer students. So, that's where the other grants came in, where we started developing new activities, new ideas, new initiatives to address those gaps. Each grant tends to serve a different level of the student population, but at the same time they overlap and build on each other.

"Having a campus-wide HSI director who coordinates our HSI leadership team has been important to ensuring campus-wide coordination that eliminates duplication of resources and efforts. It also disrupts the siloed nature of HSI work, as this work can be very isolating and confined to one area. Each year our work has evolved, and we're working strategically to combine and see how some of the grant activities can overlap with others. I'm not going to explain our HSI initiatives in detail, but you can click the QR code on the slide to visit our HSI website, which maps out the goals of each grant. You can also find information about our HSI leadership team and past events and read about our driving theories and core values. Each year we revisit these core values, and they continue to drive our work."

I reflect on Paulina's comments about having an HSI director to coordinate efforts. That is my new role, yet our campus has had five HSI grants that were not intentionally coordinated or built on each other. My first major task in this position is to document each grant's focus, objectives, and outcomes to help us understand the long-term impact and longevity of our efforts. But now Paulina also has me thinking about how they overlap and build on each other.

Paulina moves through her slides. "We have used a holistic approach to servingness, addressing various dimensions of the framework, and have embedded a racial-equity lens guided by the work of Estela Bensimon. Many of our HSI initiatives are what Gina Garcia and colleagues call 'structures for serving.' We are proud of these efforts and programs, and glad the federal government enabled us to strengthen our institutional capacity for serving Latinx students and all students of color. The funding has been used to launch educational practices that advance equitable student success and strengthen our structural capacity for serving students holistically. We have created support programs for undergraduate and graduate students, worked with community colleges to elevate transfer pathways, launched a transfer center, created a career initiative in collaboration with our Career Center, redesigned entry-level math and science courses, launched a STEM success center, and provided professional development for faculty, staff, and students on campus.

"For our indicators of servingness, we have mostly focused on enhancing academic outcomes such as increasing passing rates of gateway courses to STEM majors, increasing first-year GPAs for all Latinx students, enhancing pathways into high-paying and high-impact careers, and accelerating social mobility for Latinx students and their families. There have also been efforts to enhance what Garcia calls 'liberatory outcomes.' This has included a focus on aspirations for graduate school, sense of belonging, and financial literacy. We have also tried to embed conversations about racism and microaggressions into various programs and trainings. Since racial equity is a core focus of our HSI work, we know we have to engage in conversations about racism and white supremacy, as noted in the servingness framework."

Paulina speaks with confidence, clearly making connections between the theoretical underpinnings of servingness and her campus's HSI initiatives. I reflect on the fact that I felt lost in my HSI journey before learning about the extensive research on HSIs that guides our practice.

Paulina moves to her next slide. "We have implemented initiatives that have distinct elements from what we've seen in HSI projects on other campuses. First, we have created regional offerings, taking our HSI programs on the road to better serve students, families, and communities. We offer transitional support to incoming first-year students at our regional hubs, including writing and math workshops to help them get ready for their freshman composition course and college-level math course. These workshops are offered by faculty from our campus. We have also partnered with a community center located in a predominantly Latino neighborhood about 45 miles from the main campus, where we offer these regional programs. The community center has strong ties with the Latino community, and we have built a solid relationship with them in order to offer our college-going series in English and Spanish. This includes the math and writing workshops and workshops for families on topics such as financial aid and supporting their hijos in the transition to college. Our Title V HSI outreach coordinator plans these workshops and events. In addition to the community center, we offer similar programs at two of our community college partner sites. We believe the regional work is an important way to reach more students and their families, and to make them feel like they belong at La Playa University before they arrive.

"A second distinct element is the focus on racialized experiences in relation to the academic outcomes. Although our grant logic models and objectives are mostly focused on academic outcomes and deliverables, we have tried to provide space to have open discussions about white supremacy. For example, we offer career development through internships and workshops. Part of the internship is not only placing the students in the internship sites but also offering career coaching. The career coaching aspect means students get one-on-one meetings with the program coordinator. They also have to complete a series of modules in Canvas that have been put together by the career internship program director. As part of our partnership with the

Career Center, we helped create some of those modules to ensure they were race and identity conscious. We used that opportunity to discuss microaggressions that people of color experience in their job and internship sites, and how to navigate those better, like practices for their own mental health and how to bring this up to their mentors or supervisors. We also offer a module on professional etiquette, defining what that means and describing how that has been created and replicated by white dominant culture.

"In our efforts, we try to acknowledge students' lived experiences and are committed to preparing them to navigate the world, as they are not likely to enter Hispanic-serving companies." The crowd laughs. Paulina giggles too. "I mean, we can't fix everything, but our career internship program director has started to work with internship sites to ensure they are ready to receive and support students of color. After reading an article by Matthew Hora about college internships for Latinx students at HSIs, the HSI leadership team discussed some of the findings, including the fact that some students in that article felt like they did not fit in at their internship sites because of their race-ethnicity and gender. Latinas, in particular, felt out of place at sites where most of the interns were white men. After reading that article, we created a gender-specific career module to prepare women and transgender and nonbinary people for the workplace. We also felt it was important to talk about obstacles to full-time careers for undocumented people and successfully advocated for a module with this focus, which also includes information about navigating discrimination that immigrant and undocumented people face. Besides the career series, we also added some specific trainings and panel discussions as part of our grad school pathways HSI initiative, opening up the conversation about systemic discrimination and racism when it comes to grad school applications and how to navigate those. So, yeah, we're being intentional in our efforts to address the various ways whiteness and racism and discrimination show up along the academic and career journey.

"A final distinct dimension to our HSI work has been the ways we are creating our HSI identity, building an HSI presence, and making students aware of HSIs. We created an HSI logo and put it on T-shirts and stickers that we handed out at our campus-wide resource fair. We'd never had a table at the resource fair, which is where student organizations and campus units promote their resources, but this year we reserved a table and gave out the T-shirts and stickers. Students loved it. Now we table at all campus-wide events—we're there with our elevator pitch about HSI, and we're there just to raise awareness because students don't know that La Playa University is an HSI. They don't know what 'HSI' means and the kinds of services and programs we offer. I know when I was a student, I would often hear students ask where the HSI money was going. They would also ask why the money was not going directly to the students. So we have really tried to disrupt that through our HSI awareness campaign."

Paulina's slides are full of colorful photos of campus events with students, faculty, and staff wearing the HSI T-shirts. She scrolls through a slide with the HSI logo enlarged—it's colorful and beautiful. "We created Instagram, TikTok, and YouTube accounts for our HSI efforts, where we post information about our HSI events and share success stories of our Latinx students and faculty and staff. We also created a 90-second animated video that speaks about how La Playa University benefits from HSI grants, how students benefit, and how the funding is used. We developed the script and met with students to get feedback to make sure that they were getting the message and that it wasn't confusing. We had it translated to Spanish to make it available for family members and community members who feel more comfortable watching it in Spanish. So that video is now on our website, YouTube channel, and TikTok. We also had our student interns take over our TikTok and Instagram accounts and post about their experiences interning with the HSI grant team. We were aiming for more of a student perspective."

Benito signals to Paulina that she has two more minutes. She looks at her watch and quickly changes the slide. "One final piece of building awareness is our annual campus-wide HSI forum. The forum is a way for us to share the stories and successes of our HSI grant work. It's also a way to get the campus community engaged and informed about what we're doing and the actual impact. We also provide a space where participants can ask questions and students can offer ideas for how to better serve them. The target audience for the forums is students, so we always have food, music, and entertainment. Last year we had a local Aztec dance group perform." Paulina shows pictures from the event, then she continues. "We've hosted a series of virtual sessions to provide information to students about the new grants and how they will benefit and whatnot, but those are not as well attended as the in-person forums, probably because students do come for the food and entertainment. Overall, we believe that telling our story is so important, which is why we have focused heavily on our HSI awareness campaign. Gracias por escucharme esta mañana."

The audience claps, and Benito thanks Paulina and reminds us that there will be an open discussion after my presentation. "I know you may have questions for Paulina about her fabulous presentation, but go ahead and write those down on the Post-it notes provided and save them for our open discussion following our second presenter, Victoria. Let's give her some love this morning." The audience claps in excitement as I search for my slides.

From HSI Grants to Student-Led Movement

"Buenos días and thank you for the warm welcome. My name is Victoria, 'she,' 'her,' 'ella' pronoun series, and I am the inaugural HSI director at El Sol Community College." The audience claps for me. "I have been supporting HSI initiatives on campus for about five years and working on campus for six. I started my job with the goal of serving students one-on-one and have always been focused on holistic servingness. I think a lot of folks on campus saw that in me and pulled me into our HSI initiatives.

"My growth in servingness has been a journey, for sure. When I started working with HSI initiatives, I had very little knowledge of HSIs. I was mostly fueled by the desire to serve our Latine, low-income, and minoritized student populations on campus, with little awareness of the HSI movement, as Dr. Gina Garcia calls it. But I have since joined the movement after immersing myself in HSI research, attending HACU and AHSIE, and listening to every episode of the podcast *¿Qué pasa, HSIs?* Like most HSI practitioners, I've grappled with and continue to ask how we can center our Latine students in our HSI work. But what I have found is that it takes time. You can't expect the campus culture to change overnight. We need training, we need Gina Garcia's books, we need to learn from our sister campuses doing similar work, and we need conferences like COLEGAS to help recharge and refuel our Latine souls."

I pause as I start to get a little emotional. This really has been a journey—a beautiful journey. And I really love the work that I do. "I've prepared a few slides to guide this conversation. Like Paulina, I will share some best practices from our work at El Sol. One of the projects that I developed under one of our HSI grants and that I'm most proud of is a Latine student advisory board. By offering our students a seat at the table, the advisory board has given Latine students the platform and tools they need to be engaged in our HSI work and to challenge the status quo on our campus. It's also a place where they can feel empowered to approach their work through an antiracist, race-conscious, equity-minded, and Latinx-centered lens. We have used HSI grant funds to partner with various organizations to provide training and professional development, including the USC Race and Equity Center. A group of practitioner-scholars created a series of workshops specifically for our students, focusing on their development as student leaders and providing them with the tools they need to be equity advocates on campus. The students on the advisory board are paid through the grant, so everything they do is compensated, including the trainings they attend.

"We started with a Latine focus to align with the HSI grant activities, but we have since established a Black student advisory board and an AAPI student advisory board. Now we have three represented groups whose job is to participate in working groups and campus committees, participate in governance processes, partner with faculty to enhance curriculum and pedagogical practices, and serve as the student voice. Not just a student voice, but a critical, empowered voice. These groups are challenging the traditional ways we have done higher education, with the goal of helping our current students and reflecting on their needs. I haven't mentioned that 80% of our student population is students of color, so anything we do with HSI work has an impact on the most minoritized students who enter our campus. It's also an example of the ways that HSI work does not have to be exclusionary to Latine students, especially if you are operating through an equity-minded, antiracist lens. The three groups are working together and building a coalition grounded in justice and solidarity, not scarcity and competition. We should all learn from these students about what coalition building looks like." My slides include pictures of our students, so I pause and allow attendees to experience their joy and recognize the capital our students hold, which unfortunately is often not tapped into.

I advance to the next slide. "The campus has really embraced the student advisory boards and is starting to reach out to us for support with their own initiatives and programs. Some colleagues on campus have asked for students to table at campus events to help promote the various resources we offer, while others have asked our students to help review focus group protocols or messaging and communication that goes out to students. A more recent collaboration I'm excited to share is with the Office of Professional Development. This partnership is in the making, but we hope to create a framework for incorporating student voices in various PD activities on campus. For example, we're considering ways students can partner with faculty to enhance pedagogical practices. The idea is that student leaders would work with faculty who have opted in to have students observe a classroom or review artifacts where the teacher wants feedback. While the students are not experts in the content or subject, they are experienced in the ways they learn and engage with information presented to them. That's an idea we're considering. And it all started with the HSI grant work, since the student advisory boards are currently funded by the grant, but our hope is to institutionalize these efforts. The student advisory boards are also involved with the first-year seminar."

I stop and look at my slide before continuing. "Let me back up and talk about our curriculum redesign, which has been a part of the HSI grant work. Our project director, a true Chicana at heart, has been helping to lead conversations on curriculum design for guided-entry courses and has been helping other faculty dream about what these courses can be. She is also our first-year experience coordinator and has redesigned the first-year seminar course. She built the curriculum very strategically with critical race theory as the framework. This course previously had a growth mindset focus, but now it is more focused on building liberatory outcomes. The course introduces students to Paulo Freire, Tara Yosso, and bell hooks. Students learn about Paulo Freire's banking system of education and critical consciousness, which all connect beautifully to the concept of community cultural wealth. Throughout the course, students are empowered to consider the cultural wealth that minoritized students and their communities offer the college. Similar to La Playa, the course also addresses microaggressions, providing students with an understanding of what they are and what they look like, and providing the resources available on campus should they encounter these types of actions or behaviors.

"As key members of this grant, our student advisory boards have been a part of the review and feedback process of the first-year seminar curriculum. They have given feedback and have helped the curriculum team understand how the course can be updated and whether it is easy to navigate, especially when it was strictly online during COVID-19. They have also provided feedback on the visual appeal. Our first-year seminar has over 100 sections, so there are a lot of students that we serve through the first-year seminar, a majority of whom are students of color because of our population. So we check in with our student advisory groups to ask them whether it's too heavy or easy to read. We also want to ensure the content is something that the students feel connected to."

I pause for a moment and check in with the audience to make sure they're still with me. I see all eyes on me. I smile, advance my slides, and continue. "Another initiative the student advisory boards launched was a series of workshops. And one of the things they did is they reached out to faculty, administrators, and staff and said, 'We're creating a workshop series that is going to be Latinx-centered, and we want you to offer a workshop.' So they encouraged folks from across campus to develop content and told them that being Latinx-centered could mean many things, and they wanted to complicate what that meant. So faculty, staff, and administrators signed up, and we hosted a variety of workshops, including being first gen, being a Latinx leader, mental health and wellness, and dealing with imposter syndrome, but looking at it through a systemic lens, highlighting how systems create these imposter syndromes, because there's a lot of places where we're made to believe we don't belong. We called these workshops SOMOS El Sol to go along with our HSI identity campaign. And we felt like, OK, we can have T-shirts and stickers that say "Somos El Sol," but it didn't feel right if we didn't have a community—why have "Somos El Sol" if we don't feel it or embrace it? And so, the workshops were one way that we aimed to build community and understanding of what it means to support one another and to develop a sense of belonging. And the workshops designed by administrators, faculty, and staff were in alignment with the Latine advisory group's objectives to unify our efforts, highlight our Latinx representation, and build a culture of care and support for our Latinx students."

I stop to allow folks to see the content on my slide, which has information about our workshop series and photos of our students presenting in their Somos El Sol T-shirts. I hadn't thought about the fact that the T-shirt campaign is an awareness building campaign, but I agree with Paulina—we are building HSI awareness on campus. I continue. "An interesting thing we saw with the workshop series was that the sense of belonging wasn't just for students. It was for staff and faculty and administrators too. One staff member said to me, 'Thanks for inviting me.' Because usually we have faculty who take the lead on developing presentations or workshops, and often we see faculty as the core teachers on campus. And so we usually invite them to design or facilitate workshops. But this staff member, who was a director of a STEM program, did an amazing presentation, and she felt validated and felt a sense of belonging in that opportunity to present and share her knowledge. She felt like she belonged in the HSI work. And maybe that is something we should think about—do people feel a sense of belonging to our collective HSI work on campus?" I pause again as people snap in agreement.

"In this presentation, I've primarily focused on the area where I've had the most involvement, which is creating and overseeing the work of our student advisory boards. And I'm really proud of that work. We have many HSI successes stemming from the work with students. But I'd like to also recognize that over the years we've succeeded in being awarded multiple HSI grants, and we've launched many projects and initiatives that have contributed to our movement toward a campus-wide HSI identity. With our first Title V grant, we created a student learning center and established many programs, including extensive tutoring support. We also created a summer bridge program for new students and a first-year experience program, both of which still operate in various iterations.

"With another Title V grant, we created a continuing student experience program, which is one of the only programs dedicated to serving our second- and third-year students. It's similar to first-year experience programs in that it provides holistic support, but it is focused on our continuing students. We often give students a ton of services and support in their first year, and then it's like, 'OK, go spread your wings.' But in reality, a lot of them need more than that one year before they can fly. So that program helps students as they continue on their journeys, and they now have a support network and a space they can go to for guidance. These have all been great initiatives, and the campus is so proud of our HSI-grant-funded programs, but with each of these initiatives, we were not centering Latine students unapologetically. And that didn't sit well with our current HSI grant team.

"In the past, HSI grants were often approached as additional funding opportunities rather than as tools to meaningfully engage with the mission of serving Latine students. Historically, the process of developing these proposals did not always reflect the diverse perspectives and lived experiences of the communities these grants are meant to serve. While some efforts were made to involve Latinx voices, the depth of that inclusion often fell short, leaving room for growth in creating truly collaborative spaces where diverse perspectives could shape the work. While we're not where we need to be yet, there's a growing recognition that it's not enough to create programs that impact a large number of students if the institution itself hasn't fully embraced the work of serving Latine students.

"We're now laying the groundwork for what it truly means to serve Latine students in a way that is inclusive and intentional. Although we are still navigating this shift, these efforts are setting the stage to hold future HSI grants—and our campus—accountable to this mission. For example, we now have an HSI website and logo—neither of which existed a year ago. These might seem like small, simple changes, but they are significant. They serve as visible reminders of why we receive these grants and affirm our commitment to our identity as an HSI. By including the logo on materials and actively promoting our HSI status, the college is sending a clear message about the importance of this work and the effort it takes to truly serve our community.

"And so, the last thing I want to talk about is the creation of my position, which is in response to the need for intentional collaboration across grants, more campus-wide coordination and accountability for servingness, and a greater focus on unapologetically centering Latine students. We also think our HSI work shouldn't be based only on HSI grants, because we are an HSI regardless of the grants. So the current HSI grant team had multiple conversations about what could happen if we had a director of HSI overseeing the multiple grants as they come in, making sure that grant teams that are ending talk to those that are just starting new grants to share where they left off, even if the goals are different, and just to make sure we have a mission to center our Latine and minoritized populations. And to really hold people accountable. And although we know HSI grants do benefit all students, the group of us that advocated for an HSI director stressed that we needed to unapologetically center Latine students in our HSI work. So that is my job—to lead the HSI movement on campus, to lead with corazón as a Latina, to lead con cariño with our Latine students at the heart of all our work. And I'm excited. Thank you for listening today and showing me so much kindness throughout my presentation."

The crowd cheers as I return to my table. With big smiles, Alejandra and Susana congratulate me on my presentation.

Leading for Change, Working Against the Status Quo

10:54 a.m. Benito returns to the front of the room. "Let's thank our presenters one more time." More cheers from the group. "We are now going to have a gallery walk, followed by some discussion. You'll notice large Post-it notes around the room with some of the themes that have emerged. You've each been given small Post-it notes to write down your thoughts, ideas, and responses to the theme. I've created a slide that lists the themes to help prompt you to write down your thoughts. Once you're done, and if it is accessible to you, I invite you to walk around to each Post-it note and reflect on the theme. Here are the themes: (1) Hiring an HSI director (not a grant director), (2) redesigning curriculum, (3) implementing HSI student advisory groups, (4) building HSI awareness, (5) creating HSI logos and T-shirts, (6) working with the region, (7) working with Latine community centers, (8) embedding critical perspectives in first-year experience courses, (9) infusing conversations about microaggressions into all programs, (10) building solidarity, and (11) professional development.

"I came up with these themes based on my review of the presentations, but does anyone have any additional contributions?"

There is a brief moment of silence before one person raises their hand. "I heard the word 'liberatory' more than once—can we make that a theme? My campus does not use that word in our HSI work, so I would love to talk more about it."

Benito nods in agreement. "Yes, let's add that theme. I'll make another Post-it note while y'all work on your responses. Anything else?" Benito pauses and allows time for silence. They continue, "I'll also create a Post-it paper for open ideas, in case you have other thoughts that don't align with these themes."

11:01 a.m. I reflect on the themes that both Paulina and I offered to the group. I find it interesting how we talked about similar things, but I also learned new things from her. I grab the orange Post-it notes, to match my dress, and jot down some ideas. I hadn't thought about creating online modules for trainings and professional development, but I think that might be a way to reach more faculty and staff on campus. We could create servingness modules that faculty and staff are required to complete, although I'm not yet sure how we would hold them accountable. I write this idea down in my journal, as I want to think about it when I get back to campus. People begin to walk around the room, adding their sticky notes to the larger Post-its. I do the same once I'm done jotting notes. We spend time moving around the room, conversing with each other as we participate in the activity. Benito reminds us to take our time at each thematic Post-it paper and read what our colleagues have added to the notes. After about 30 minutes, Benito asks us to return to our seats for more discussion.

Benito opens up the talk. "We have about 30 minutes to continue to share ideas based on what we heard from our presenters and what we saw during the gallery walk. This is a space for idea generation and knowledge exchange. If you have new ideas to contribute, please share freely with the group. We would love to hear what is happening on other campuses that aligns with the themes we have identified."

One person immediately raises their hand.

Using Spanish Is Liberatory But Also Invites Racism

"Hola a todos, I'm Oscar, a grant director at an HSI community college, and I want to thank Paulina and Victoria for your insightful presentations. I took a lot of notes and shared many thoughts on the Post-its. One thing I want to talk about is the liberation piece. I saw a lot of ideas on that theme as I walked around, and I think it's something we need to think about. What does liberation in HSIs look like? At my campus, we developed a space to build community and decided to call it El Centro. But it was a struggle to get people to buy in to that name because the writers of the grant tried to whitewash our HSI grant. So we put names on our HSI like Transfer PREP, with the PREP being an acronym for something that I can't even remember." People giggle and nod. "And so anything we did as a grant, we had to label

Transfer PREP, and I'm like, no, hell no, we're going to name this HSI Center or whatever, because I really wanted the image to be front and center.

"So we created El Centro, and it was the first Spanish name on our campus. But it was a whole revolt. People who wrote the grant were upset because they didn't want the name to be in Spanish. Nevertheless, we pushed forward, and we created this space. And that is liberatory to me. For our Hispanic students to see the center's name in Spanish is liberatory. We also embedded supports for undocumented students within that space, but we had to do that undercover because our campus was not supportive of it. We also weren't able to use federal funds specifically for undocumented students. So we just tried to create a space that was welcoming to all our Hispanic students, regardless of their status or background. And it seems so basic, but these are things that our campus has not had or done before.

"We also hired Spanish-speaking counselors that had a mental health background or psychology background. So that was another thing we did because we were noticing a need. We did a survey of our students that came into the summer bridge program—it was an anonymous survey—and 60% of our students identified that they had mental health problems or that they had mental health concerns. When I graduated high school, I didn't know about mental health. In addition, 48% of those students identified that they were caretakers to either a child or a parent. Man, these kids are 18 years old and they're taking care of a parent or a child or a sister or brother. And so of course we had a great team, and we quickly realized, hey, guys, I think the focus—we do want to focus on retention, trust me, I know we're here for academics, but I think we need to focus on the mental health of these students. So we implemented a lot of programming with mental health, with student health services, just because we needed it. There was also a spike in fentanyl overdosing in our community.

"So all those things, of course they were important, and then you add the pandemic in the middle of everything. So I think at that point, we were just responding to the crisis. Even though we wanted to be intentional in our servingness, our retention rates were not the best for students, but if they had to leave college for a little bit or put a hold on their academics, we made sure that they were taken care of mentally, spiritually, and so on. So that has been a big focus. And just acknowledging that not every day it's going to be sunny, and that we have to be okay with that. And that we have to sometimes push through those gloomy days. So we've been doing a lot of that kind of thing. And that is liberatory—to just acknowledge our students' humanity is liberatory for them. Because if they're hungry, or they have to take care of a child or a parent or someone else, or they're having a gloomy day, then they can't do well in their classes, and we won't meet our academic outcome goals. And so I agree that liberatory outcomes are measures of HSI success—students' positive mental health is an indicator of success. Pero the white people on campus just don't get it. And they are the people writing the grants. And so, as the director, it's also been a form of resistance and liberation for me to implement what I know our Hispanic students need."

The crowd snaps in agreement. Benito chimes in. "Yeeeess, Oscar. I love the conversation on the use of Spanish in our HSI work and the focus on mental health. Thank you for sharing. Any other ideas from the group?"

Financial Literacy Is Important But Insufficient

"Hello, everyone. My name is Michelle—'she,' 'her' pronouns—and I am an HSI grant director at a community college. I appreciate everything that has been shared so far. One thing Paulina mentioned but didn't go into detail about, and there wasn't a Post-it note for, was financial literacy. I'm glad to hear that other campuses are adding financial literacy to their HSI programming. That is one of the liberatory outcomes we're focused on with our HSI grant, creating programming that will lead to financial literacy. So we added that component to our first-year experience, with things like 'How do you do FAFSA? When do you do FAFSA? What documents do you need?' We also talked about ways to save, especially when students get a $1,000 or $2,000 refund, talking about putting it away. But here's the thing—we knew that in order for this to be successful, we had to take into consideration that Latinx students don't come to financial literacy in a vacuum. It's hard to think about saving money and being financially literate when you're living paycheck to paycheck. And that's the reality. When you're hearing Mom and Dad talk about 'How do we keep the lights on?' Or when you're worried about how *you* keep the lights on, when you're making choices between 'Do we buy food, or do we buy prescriptions, or do we get propane?' Or 'Oh my gosh, I just got garnished,' or 'Oh my gosh, child support's coming out now,' or 'I'm not getting child support.' That's all reality.

"So it's really easy to talk about saving and talk about doing things, but the bottom line is that's not real life for our Latinx students. So while I'm glad financial literacy is in our grant, I think we need to meet students where they are and say 'Sometimes scraping by is the best you can do, and here's some things to try.' I think we need to break it down into smaller bites because Latinx students, rural students, students of color, we don't always have that saving option. You can't save money out of a paycheck that doesn't exist or a paycheck that is already short. And so I wanted to add that to our conversation, that sometimes what sounds good in the grant doesn't translate in real life for the students we are serving."

Folks around the room nod, and some snap, acknowledging this is the reality of our servingness work.

Oscar raises his hand and jumps back into the conversation. "Michelle, thanks for bringing this up. We also noticed our students were struggling financially. Last year a lot of my students who were single parents were having car trouble, and I was reading articles about how single parents really do struggle a lot with car repairs. And students were asking me things like 'Hey, how do I buy a car?' Or 'This car has been passed down to me, now what do I need to do?' So we brought in a local financial consultant. She's super amazing, and she talked about a couple of areas. First, white credit is racist and what you can do about it. Second, finance 101 for communities of color and budgeting for low-income communities. So things that are really tailored to our Latino and low-income students. And we sent the students an assessment with simple questions like 'Do you have a savings account today?' And then the post-assessment asked things like 'Did you create a savings account?' or 'Did we facilitate the process for you to create one?' So we are assessing the impact of the financial literacy workshops. I like what you said about things like savings accounts being out of reach for some of our students, because it's true. But we took the approach of, like, building their financial literacy is a win, even if they can't build their financial wealth at the moment. So for us, financial literacy really is about building their knowledge about budgeting, saving, investing, and stuff like that, even if they can't use that knowledge just yet."

Michelle nods. "I like that part about white credit is racist! I am going to take that back to my grant team and see if we can talk about that too. Thanks for sharing that. You're right, building financial literacy and knowledge is empowering for low-income students and students of color, and we were jumping into financial wealth building, which they might not be ready for. While I have the floor, I will add that we're sending faculty to ESCALA for professional development this summer. We have six faculty members, and I was blunt with them and told them, 'There will be work before, work during, and work after. And your job is to get uncomfortable and then make other people on campus uncomfortable, and to do it until it's not uncomfortable anymore.' And I was surprised—I got a lot of positive responses from faculty who are willing to do that. Leadership, not so much. Faculty on campus, yeah. The folks who are in the classrooms, who are talking to students every day in their offices are wanting to do that and are looking forward to picking a project, which is what ESCALA asked us to do to move forward. So those are the things we're working on."

Culturally Responsive Pedagogies But Not in STEM

Benito thanks Michelle for her comments. "We have time for one more story from the group. Yes, Dra. Zapata, go ahead."

"Hello, everyone, I am Dra. Zapata, and I work with Benito here on campus. I spent most of my time at the Post-it note theme of redesigning curriculum. I wanted to see what other campuses are doing because we've had some successes and some setbacks in that part of our HSI work. A major part of our Title V grant is working on culturally responsive pedagogy and specifically creating support for faculty who want to innovate and change their curriculum. One of the things we have recognized is that there are a lot of faculty who are excited and want to do things different, but they don't know how or don't understand how to change what they've been doing for a long time. So our efforts really have been focused on trying to get culturally responsive pedagogy and curriculum into our instruction. One of the things we have come to realize on our campus is that it's really difficult to just require everyone to change their curriculum, and not everyone is going to get on board, but if we can find those champions who are wanting to innovate, then we can help them in their courses to do that. And it's a model for other faculty to look at. We're also working on an equity audit that can show some of those courses where our diverse students may not be succeeding, and we're trying to pinpoint that a little more, which is scary for faculty. So we're trying to look at what is being done differently in those courses where students are succeeding and not trying to call out individuals.

"We also hired two instructional coaches to work with faculty on curriculum redesign—one was working with science, and one was working with English. And they had a team of faculty they worked with, doing book studies, looking at high-impact practices, exploring the research, all of that coming into play in their course redesign. And then they redesigned the course, and the faculty that decided to implement the curriculum then would also be paid extra, out of the Title V grant funds, to be able to implement those kinds of things. But science faculty are, let's say, tricky, and we stopped working with the science department because frankly they were just not ready. And they said they'd been harmed by the work, but they were actually harming my instructional coaches. So I pulled them out of there and just didn't allow it to continue—but the work was good. I mean, we have data to prove the students who were in courses that had curriculum redesign, they actually did better. Their performance metrics—GPA and completion—were higher than the students in courses that didn't have the redesign. And so we had proof that it was working. So it is disappointing that we had to stop our work with the science department, which is where a lot of our students struggle. So what I guess I'm asking for is colleagues who might want to sit together at lunch today to talk about strategies for engaging resistant faculty in this work, because we need them on board, but they aren't always willing."

At my table, Alejandra raises her hand and says, "I'll join you. I'm having the same problem on my campus."

Another voice from the back of the room yells, "Yo también." We all laugh.

Benito speaks again. "Thank you all for this engaging conversation. As you can see, we are all doing very cool and very important work, but it's not all rainbows and sunshine. We all face some challenges, and that's why we are here—to share stories and support each other. Please continue to review the themes on the wall and add more thoughts. We'll type these up and send them to the group afterward. Disfruta del almuerzo y vuelve aquí a la 1:00 p.m."

Categorizing Change

12:43 p.m. After lunch, I spend time outside under a tree reflecting on the morning. I take notes in my journal. I'm thankful to be here with my colleagues and to learn with them. I draw a table with three columns and jot down some notes about the different types of change we discussed today (see table 2.1).

We discussed a lot of changes to the infrastructure, which is a common way that campuses use HSI grants—launch a Title V–sponsored center for transfer students, or for STEM, or for Latine students, or redesign curriculum, or create a Spanish-language family orientation program. But the more innovative approach to infrastructure transformation is to hire an HSI director to oversee all the HSI work, although that does require campus resources beyond the grants. At El Sol, we advocated for a campus HSI director for over a year and put a lot of pressure on administration to fund the position. Our work adding critical perspectives to the first-year experience course is a

Table 2.1
Changes Influenced by HSI Grants

Changes to the Campus Infrastructure (First-Order Change)	Changes to Processes (First-Order and Second-Order Change)	Changes to Individual Mindsets and Campus Culture/Institutional Logics (Second-Order Change)
Launch a transfer center.	Create transfer pathways from community college to four-year institution.	Provide HSI-specific professional development for educators and leaders on campus.
Launch a STEM success center.	Develop cross-disiciplinary collaboration to create new STEM initiatives.	Build solidarity in the HSI movement across racial/ethnic groups.
Launch a cultural center.	Collaborate with a local Latine community center to launch programs.	Make annual training about racism and microaggressions mandatory for all employees.
Initiate a Spanish-language orientation.	Invite student advisory members to work with faculty on course (re) design.	Create an HSI identity and HSI branding.
Redesign entry-level courses (math, English, science).	Connect HSI grants over time; build on previous HSI grants.	Train student leaders to be HSI advocates.
Hire Spanish-speaking counselors.	Hire HSI director to lead HSI change-management efforts.	Use HSI grants to create liberatory experiences.
Launch HSI student advisory group.	Embed critical theory into first-year seminar.	

change to the curriculum infrastructure, but it ultimately changes students' mindsets, so it could fit into multiple categories.

Some of the changes we discussed today are changes to processes or approaches we use. This includes working with partner institutions to create transfer pathways, collaborating with other departments on campus, or partnering with community organizations. These things may lead to changes in the infrastructure, but it really is about the partnerships and processes that drive those changes. Paulina described the ways her HSI grants built on each other to elevate various components, which is something our campus hasn't done well, with each grant operating in a silo. So that is a process I want to work on in my new role as HSI director.

I think the most dramatic changes are those that lead to new individual mindsets and new institutional logics. Training and professional development really fits into this category, but I think it has to be intentionally critical. When our students went through equity and antiracism training, their mindsets changed dramatically. They learned to vocalize injustices they were seeing and had the language to call out inequities. And now they're advocating for equity and justice in various governance and decision-making spaces across campus, which should lead to a change in institutional culture and institutional logics—at least I hope so. Our HSI branding has also changed institutional logics as our colleagues across campus are starting to embrace our HSI identity. They want our shirts and stickers. They want to represent our HSI identity. These adaptations are shifting the campus culture to one of strategy and intention.

I stop writing and take a few minutes to enjoy the sun. It's been a good day so far. I look forward to the second half of the meeting.

3

Processes of Servingness

How we live and grow and stay purposeful in the face of constant change actually does determine both the quality of our lives, and the impact that we can have when we move into action together.
—adrienne maree brown, *Emergent Strategy: Shaping Change, Changing Worlds* (2017)

BOTH THE SERVINGNESS FRAMEWORK (Garcia et al., 2019a) and the transforming HSIs framework (Garcia, 2023) give researchers and practitioners a way to assess institutional capacity for serving Latine students and a guide to drive organizational transformation. The servingness framework provided us with the terminology "structures for serving," which are the palpable dimensions of colleges and universities that enable HSIs to adequately serve Latine students. These include mission and values statements; diversity plans; HSI grants; institutional advancement activities; engagement with the Latine community; compositional diversity of faculty, staff, administrators, and graduate students; culturally relevant curriculum and pedagogy; programs and services for minoritized students; leadership and decision-making practices; incentive structures; and external boundary management (Garcia et al., 2019a). The T-HSI framework includes the same dimensions as well as organizational identity, strategic purpose, physical infrastructure, governance structures, families, alumni, and local communities (Garcia, 2023). With both frameworks, I argue that HSIs must *change* the structures for serving, or the infrastructure, in order to actualize an HSI identity and embody servingness. Yet I do not distinguish the actual *processes of change*, or what I am calling "*processes of servingness.*"

Other HSI scholars and practitioners have similarly been writing about servingness and in some cases describing the tasks and activities they are engaging in to change their structures for serving, yet they have not called them "processes" either. Notably, Franco and Muñiz (2022) argued the servingness framework "stimulate[s] critical reflection and guide[s] thoughtful and responsive action" (p. 99), which may be essential servingness processes. They further note the framework can be used as a tool of "institutional assessment to determine the scope and depth at which HSIs substantively and effectively serve Latinx students" (Franco & Muñiz, 2022, p. 101), with assessment also being an important servingness process. Franco and Muñiz also lay out a series of tasks and activities that their campuses undertook as part of their servingness journey. For the University Arizona, these tasks included collecting and reflecting on data, making presentations on campus about the data, launching visioning forums, and critically examining incentive structures such as faculty promotion and tenure processes. For the University of Central Florida, activities included launching a task force in the initial planning stages, engaging with external organizations such as Excelencia in Education for technical guidance on data collection and disaggregation, providing professional development for faculty, creating a faculty hiring toolkit, hosting HSI book clubs, and sponsoring HSI Week activities.

Petrov and Garcia (2021) also laid out specific processes of organizational change and described how Title V grant funds can be used to support the campus's transformation toward an ethos of servingness. They suggested that campuses engage in conversations about whiteness, coloniality, and intersectionality to disrupt systems of oppression that hinder equitable outcomes. Other activities and tasks that Dominican University partook in include hiring people of color to provide professional development, sending a faculty cohort to training with ESCALA Educational Services, and creating a Truth,

Racial Healing, and Transformation Center. These processes specifically engaged outside organizations, which is a part of the servingness framework. Petrov and Garcia (2021) also noted that grassroots leaders on campus drove some of the change processes, such as chairing committees to implement policy change.

McNaughtan and Lujan (2023) interviewed presidents of HSI community colleges to assess how leaders support and ensure servingness. Some of the core processes they described include increasing representation of Latine faculty to align with the student population, developing training for faculty and staff on how to best support students, preparing future leaders for the institution, and developing specific services for the Latine community. Others have argued that aligning the campus's strategic plans with HSI commitments and naming Latine students within the strategic plan are essential servingness processes (Flores & Leal, 2023). Villarreal Sosa et al. (2023) claimed a critically reflexive process on governance and leadership is essential for disrupting racial and political dynamics of decision-making and traditional notions of faculty governance. Some campuses have also asked students for feedback in focus groups (Velez et al., 2024). There are numerous examples of how educators and leaders at HSIs are engaging in processes of change to transform their campus cultures and institutional logics in ways that embrace servingness and a Latine-serving identity. If the stated goal of the campus is to become an HSI, or to embody a Latine-serving identity, the campus must implement new tasks, activities, and processes to meet that goal.

Processes of servingness can be observed within HSI contexts but may also be witnessed on campuses that are actively working toward the 25% (eHSIs). Some of these eHSIs are engaging in processes of change as they prepare to reach the 25% although not all of them. Striving HSIs (sHSIs) that enroll below 15% Latine students are also engaging in processes of change. The key is to move with intention toward growth and regeneration (brown, 2017). Emergent strategy calls on us to embrace change as constant while remaining purposeful. Campuses that plan for the shift in demographics know change is inevitable, and they strategically plan for it rather than become irrelevant in the face of change (brown, 2017).

Witnessing How Institutions Intentionally Adapt

The next counterstory is about institutions that are figuring out how to be HSIs regardless of the 25% enrollment threshold of Latine students and regardless of eligibility and federal HSI grant seeking and getting. These colleges and universities are noticing the growing population of Latine college students and committing to the HSI designation. This counterstory is also about intentional adaptation, or the strategic ways the campus responds to its students, and it is narrated by Nayeli, a reporter who writes for a higher education newspaper that publishes news, information, and opinions about US colleges and universities. Her editor asked her to write a story for HSI Week, which is a weeklong celebration of HSIs. She's excited to cover the topic after writing an article about Minority Serving Institutions in Chicago a few years ago. She learned a lot while researching that story, and she looks forward to learning more. In preparing for this next story, Nayeli came across a few news articles and blogs about HSIs and servingness—a new concept to her, but from what she's read, servingness seems to be about transforming organizational structures to better serve Latine students and about the ways campuses can measure change through academic and liberatory outcomes (Garcia, 2019, December; Garcia, 2020, May; Garcia, 2021). Nayeli has also learned about campuses that have been recognized with the Seal of Excelencia. But because she's a fierce advocate for the underdog, she has decided to highlight in her article some campuses that have not been recognized with any honors or HSI clout.

Learning About Striving, Emerging, and Eligible HSIs

Nayeli has scheduled three interviews for her story. The first is with a woman named Lily who's employed at a four-year private university that has been working to become an HSI for several years (sHSI). The second interview is with a woman named Eli who works at a four-year private emerging HSI (eHSI). Nayeli learned through a quick search that there are 412 emerging HSIs in the United States, a number that represents 13% of all colleges and universities in the country, and so she's decided this is an important HSI category to highlight (Excelencia in Education, 2024). And finally, Nayeli is also scheduled to speak with Taylor, a woman who works at a two-year eligible HSI community college.

Strategic Intentions Don't Require Grants

Tuesday morning. I'm running behind today. My son woke up late and missed the bus, so I had to battle two miles of traffic in Chicago to drive him to school. And then two miles back. Most days I wake up, shower, put on stretchy pants and a cute shirt—for any Zoom calls later in the day—and then I drink my coffee on the front porch. I get to watch the hustle and bustle of the morning pass by while I enjoy the fact that I've been working from home since the COVID-19 pandemic. It's a good life. Today has been a little more hectic than normal, but now I'm ready for my interview with Lily.

I enter the Zoom room where she's already waiting. "Hello, Lily. Thank you for agreeing to talk to me today."

She quickly unmutes herself. "Hi, Nayeli. Thanks for reaching out. I love to talk about HSIs, so thank you for the invitation."

"As I mentioned in my email," I begin, "I'm writing a story about HSIs for HSI Week. Are you OK with me recording this interview?" Lily nods. "Great," I say. "Can you start by telling me about your role in HSI work on your campus?"

"Sure. My role was created to help steward our campus to become a Hispanic Serving Institution. I spent the first year getting the lay of the land, getting to know the community, doing a giant SWOT analysis, and putting forward some recommendations to the administration around what we would need to do, not just to increase our Latinx student enrollment but also to ensure that students could really thrive here. At the time, we had a very low percentage of Hispanic undergrads. We had quite a way to go on all those fronts. In terms of what I do, I guess, what don't I do in terms of the HSI initiative?" She laughs. "I've developed community relationships. I do precollege stuff. I run a mentorship program with our local high school and some of our students. I work with faculty on programming and support different academic programs.

"For example, I have a dotted line to Ethnic Studies. I work very closely with our Student Life Division to develop programming that supports and enhances the experience of our underrepresented students. I've had connections with our Hispanic Alumni Association. So I do a little bit of everything when it comes to HSI. The way I see my role is that of the person who thinks about this all the time and pushes at the edges to make things happen, collaborates with colleagues, convenes the right people, and listens to the right stories to move the needle."

I take notes as Lily speaks, but I'm glad I'm also recording this conversation.

Lily continues. "I feel like we've moved the needle in a number of different spheres. In the beginning, we had an HSI advisory team, and that group helped me to develop the SWOT analysis. And when I presented the SWOT analysis to the provost, they were like, 'Wow, this is so great. This is a lot of good information, really good recommendations. We don't have any money, so maybe next year we can follow up. But is there any low-hanging fruit we can start working on?' And certainly there was. For example, we were able to put together a website for undergrads in Spanish. We have 60 to 65 pages translated into Spanish with really key information that families would want to know. And then we were able to hire Spanish speakers in key roles in admissions and financial aid. There were some other changes that didn't require resources but required leadership to make them happen. And so I was able to get in the right rooms and talk to the right people to help move these things forward."

I jump in. "When you say you were doing things that didn't require resources, do you mean monetary resources? Because it seems the things you have been able to do require human resources you already have. Is that accurate?"

"Yes, that is correct," Lily says. "We used the human resources we already had and accessed support from our leaders. We absolutely needed our administrators to support the work."

"OK, thanks for clarifying," I say. "That's an important distinction in times of fiscal uncertainty for campuses. From what I understand, many HSIs are focused on getting grants in order to serve Latine students, but you're suggesting that HSIs can do this work without grants or funds."

Lily nods. "Absolutely. And in our case, we are not eligible for Title V grants because we do not have 25% Latine students yet. Last fall we finally hit that emerging HSI mark. We were just over 15% enrollment. And every year we've grown our Latinx and underrepresented student enrollment in our freshman class. My understanding is that one-third of our population is students of color, which is wonderful for us as a historically white institution. We have made progress. But interestingly, if you look at our rate of growth, it's slowing. In the beginning, we were making really, really big gains. And over time, we've made smaller and smaller gains. And so, if we continue on this current trajectory, we're not going to hit that 25%.

"Just in terms of the eligibility criteria for HSI, that's a concerning thing for me. I believe it's in large part due to the cost of attending a private institution. Like most universities, we don't meet full demonstrated need. A lot of our students are low-income students, and they commute from home because we don't include room and board with most of our scholarship programs. And for those who would be coming from farther away, unless they're part of one of our full scholarship programs, the cost of room and board is often prohibitive. Every year, we break records with the number of students of color we admit and the number of Latinx students we admit. But still, there are students who want to be here, who deserve to be here, who've worked really, really hard to be here, but they just can't attend because of financial reasons. That, to me, is the biggest issue."

I'm moved by this account, reflecting on my own college-going process and remembering how my family and I had trouble understanding the difference between the sticker price and the actual cost to attend. I ultimately enrolled in a private institution but commuted to campus for financial reasons. "Thank you for that insight, Lily. The process of becoming an HSI seems like a lot of work when it's intentional. Some articles I've read suggest that HSIs become HSIs accidentally without even trying. But you're suggesting that is not always the case. Can you tell me more about the outreach and admissions work you've done to increase enrollment of students of color?"

Lily smiles with excitement. "Well, I've had an amazing partnership with our dean of undergraduate admissions. And the HSI initiative had already been announced when they came on board, and it was actually part of their interview process. So it's been such a wonderful partnership in that we strategized a lot—especially in the very beginning—around what we need to do better in our office of admissions. One of the simple things was that our admissions counselors weren't even going to every local public school in our city. And it's like, this is the community that we serve. Why are we not even engaging all the schools right here in our city? We've made substantial progress on that front but still have more work to do. By definition, we are a national university, but 70% of our students come from within a two-hour drive to campus. We needed to do better to target high-performing, highly diverse schools in our metropolitan feeder regions and then be very attentive to our local community. That was part of the strategy.

"I know the financial aid strategy has also changed. I'm not privy to all the ins and outs of how they allocate financial aid, but I know they've adjusted the way we do it to attract more underrepresented students. And that has been very intentional. And I think another part of this is just the way we market ourselves and the way we understand ourselves as an increasingly diverse institution. For a long time, we've catered very comfortably to a white, upper middle class, suburban set. And that's just been our reality for decades and decades, centuries really. For us to reimagine who we are and who we could be, I think, has been a large part of not just our recruitment strategy and our admissions strategies but also how we think about all our systems and processes on campus and the ways we welcome students who come from underrepresented backgrounds."

I pause briefly to gather my thoughts before I unmute myself again. "So it sounds like your campus focuses on admissions and recruitment as a part of your HSI work?"

"Yes," Lily says, "that is an essential part of servingness for us as an emerging HSI—we must hit that 25% mark. But I don't want to overshadow the fact that a lot of our work is focused on getting the campus ready to welcome the Latinx students we are so heavily recruiting. When HSI first came out as an initiative, and this was before I was hired, but if you go back and listen to the media stuff that happened around it, to the radio interviews with university administration, there was a lot of focus on enrollment numbers. And there was a lot of focus on admissions. There was very little conversation about what happens when you bring these students to campus. And so, to me, an important part of what I had to do—and in fact a surprising amount of my time, especially in the first year or two—was around changing the narrative. Because there was already this perception out there that all HSI means is getting these numbers. And it seemed like the students felt tokenized, like it's just a statistic. And Black students and Indigenous students also felt like, well, what about us? We're left out of this.

"And so we had to reimagine and rethink the way we were talking about HSI and what it means. This was before the idea of servingness became a thing. We had to make this up. And because there was no model, I called institutions that had recently become HSIs, and they were like, 'Yeah, it was accidental, happenstance kind of thing.' I could not find people who—I couldn't find research—I couldn't find any information on how you do this in a very intentional way. So we decided to be intentional in our own way. And I think our website tries to show that—that this is what we're putting out to the community around what our HSI narrative is. I can share the link with you if you want."

I nod. "That would be helpful, thanks. So you focused on recruitment and enrollment, developed a SWOT analysis, had leadership support from the highest levels, created your own HSI narrative, and developed an HSI website, to name a few efforts. Are there any other things you'd like to share?"

"Oh, yeah. We've done so many things!" Lily smiles. "I'll highlight just a few important changes we've made. In collaboration with our Belonging and Inclusion Office, we've created opportunities for our faculty and staff to learn more about issues related to racism, white supremacy, implicit bias, microaggressions, things of that nature as a personal or professional development opportunity. So hundreds of people have engaged with our programs, and they have self-reported very positive outcomes. For example, people say, 'After having gone through this particular program, I am better equipped to address microaggressions in my classroom when I see it,' or things like that. Now, does that trickle down to student experience? That's still unclear. I guess we'll find out in our next climate survey.

"We administered a survey before a lot of these educational programs were in place, and it showed lots of racial microaggressions and other microaggressions based on other social identities—women, people of color, low income, first gen, LGBTQ, people with disabilities, all have these disproportionately negative experiences on campus. We know this is here, and this is something we talk about a lot. But because we're so decentralized and because microaggressions are often subtle, they persist and proliferate. We've tried to do a lot of education. But oftentimes it's the people who are already interested in these topics who are the ones who show up. It tends to be preaching to the choir, but not always. I feel like there are people who are open to it and wanna learn and have lots of legitimate questions like 'How do I or did I commit microaggressions?' I think there's good work being done with it. It's just it's not reaching all the corners of the campus it needs to.

"We also made changes to our hiring practices, although that's another interesting thing—made mostly of add-ons. We're not fundamentally changing the way we hire faculty because it's very, very local to departments, very, very decentralized. We're encouraging new equity-focused protocols, but we're not mandating them. And this is something I worked with our HR team on, creating implicit-bias workshops around how implicit bias shows up in every single step of the hiring process, where you can interrupt it, and how you can pay closer attention to being intentional about this.

"Some departments have taken us up on this, some have not. But how we've actually moved the needle is through cluster hires. We started cluster hires for our Ethnic Studies program, and we did several years of cluster hires. This was very intentional on the part of the provost, who worked closely with the deans and department chairs to see where open faculty lines could align with this program. It took leadership, and it took resources to get that kind of authority piece. That work has since fizzled. And it's unclear whether the cluster hires will be restarted. But, I mean, we were very intentional about the kinds of fields and disciplines we targeted, and most of the scholars in those fields are people of color. So the new scholars we brought in were mostly people of color too. And our numbers of faculty of color shot up really quickly. These are all tenure track positions. Again, this shows how we're adding on but not necessarily fundamentally changing structures." Lily pauses and sips her water. "Do you want me to keep going? I can talk about this all day." We both laugh.

"Yes, please do," I say.

"Absolutely. So another change we made is to the curriculum. We're not redesigning—again, when we talk about changes, we're not actually changing the structure. We're doing a lot of add-ons. And that, to me, has been the most challenging part of our initiative. We're not changing the structure, we're not requiring Ethnic Studies for our students, but we are adding an Ethnic Studies program that students can opt into. There are things like that where, yes, progress is being made, and I think it's better than it was before, but fundamentally we're not actually changing the experience. For example, if you wanted to avoid ever talking about race or ethnicity on our campus, you could. That's the crux of it. We're in the development stages of our Ethnic Studies program, and the program leaders have done a lot of work to try to figure out what curricular pieces already fold into this and how they can build a stepwise curriculum where there will be minors and majors, and we can make sure our Latinx Studies and African American Studies and Indigenous Studies programs can work together, in tandem. That's the work. And then there's a lot of cocurricular programming that's coming out as well, but that's the academic stuff." Lily pauses before saying, "I think I'll stop there."

I unmute and thank Lily. "I appreciate you sharing so openly and willingly. This has been really helpful, and you gave me a lot to work with. I don't want to take any more of your time, so I'll go ahead and stop recording now. I'll let you know when the story will be published."

Lily smiles, thanks me in return, and waves goodbye.

The Challenges of Fractured Adaptation

Wednesday afternoon. I'm working on my story and adding the insights Lily shared with me. I did some more research before today's upcoming interview with a woman named Eli. I'm struck by how little I know about HSIs. When I wrote about Amarillo Private University (APU) in Chicago a few years back (Garcia, 2019), the story was about what HSIs do and how that campus was focused on serving Spanish-speaking Latine students and the Chicago Latine community. But APU had already historically been doing those things. I hadn't clearly realized that point until I'd talked to Lily and she'd shared how colleges and universities can *become* HSIs when they are still predominantly white institutions. The processes for these distinct kinds of institutions seem very different. Now I jot down my questions for Eli.

I enter the Zoom room, and Eli is already waiting for me. "Hi, Eli," I say warmly. "How are you?"

She looks up and smiles. "Hola, Nayeli. Estoy bien, ¿cómo estás?"

I smile too. "I'm great! Thanks for agreeing to talk to me today."

"You're welcome."

"As I mentioned, I'm writing a story about HSIs for HSI Week. Are you OK with me recording this interview?" Eli says yes, and I jump to the first question. "Can you start by telling me about how you are doing HSI work on your campus?"

"Sure. I'm the director of Hispanic initiatives at a small private university. My position was created to help the university become a Hispanic Serving Institution. Prior to my being hired, there was a task force that was convened to really help the university move forward in these initiatives. And then the university began using endowment funds for different initiatives to help increase Hispanic enrollment and retention. My position was created out of those endeavors. So I came on board one year ago, and I've been really tasked with building an office for Hispanic services and initiatives and really taking it to heart to become an HSI. I have a year under my belt now, and the year primarily has been about educating faculty and staff about HSI as a concept, the term, the history of HSIs, stuff like that.

"Now I'm working on creating programming for Hispanic students. I work under the chief diversity officer, who implemented a strategic plan for the university to become more diverse and to create a sense of belonging for all students. Her strategic plan had different areas of growth for the university, and becoming an HSI was a big area of growth. So I sit under that office, which has a student-facing side that oversees our first-gen scholars' programs. We have a summer bridge program, and we do mentorship for students. We used to run a food pantry out of that center and a book-lending program, but in early fall, those programs were taken on by other departments in the university. So they've actually expanded their services and are more open to all students. We're happy they have outgrown our space. We're happy we were part of starting it and now handing it off and seeing its growth. So, yes, that's a little bit about my role and what it entails."

I unmute myself to ask a follow-up question. "Is your role more about providing Hispanic student services or about HSI? Your campus is not an HSI yet, is that correct?"

"That is correct—we are an emerging HSI. Becoming an HSI was part of the university's strategic plan, but at the same time, the university had decided we were going to start these different initiatives for diversity. They wanted to address declining enrollment. The big trade-off was that the university decided to dip into our endowment to really help grow our enrollment. I think there were different folks at the table deciding on different initiatives. There were a few that were started for veterans, and other different populations. Then the VP of enrollment took on HSI and said, 'I think this is the direction we need to run in.' So he was the one that was chairing the task force before I came on board. He was overseeing all of enrollment and marketing, which is a big deal in our space.

"For our institution, 90% of our budget comes from student tuition. A big part of the budget that's used every year goes to marketing and enrollment. So I think it was a big deal that the VP was the one taking charge of the HSI initiative, because he also has a lot of players at hand that could move things on the ground. And because the drive came from the marketing and enrollment side, they really wanted to focus on that when I began. As the task force was convened and started to grow in their research and in their plans, they hired an outside consultant to really determine what the image was of the institution in the local community. And because we're a faith-based institution, I laughed at the way they started their research. Initially, it was about how the Catholic Hispanic population perceives us as a Christian institution. I was like, 'Well, that's already starting off wrong.' I was like, 'If you already know your target population, then start there. Don't create more barriers than needed in the research.' So the results came back—I mean the focus groups and the interviews they did with folks—and a lot of people said, 'We don't know anything about this school.' So there was a push to start a campaign, especially under the VP's leadership. He felt like that was the biggest priority. So it became about this Spanish campaign. By the time I came on, that campaign was ready to launch. The first month I was here, they hosted a Spanish radio station.

"A lot of people came out. It was a great event. But after that event, when I talked to the marketing folks, I said, 'I think we're not ready because you don't have any Spanish-speaking admissions counselors. If you call the front desk, no one knows any Spanish.' For this radio event, if people had questions, they were directed to the Spanish teachers, which makes sense because they helped organize the event, but it didn't make sense in that it was an event hosted by the university. It wasn't hosted by the Spanish teachers. So we halted that campaign, and then I decided we needed to focus on other areas of growth. We're not there yet. We don't have the infrastructure to invite more

Hispanic students when students already here are not receiving support—or we're not even ready to receive a phone call."

I'm struck by this statement. "What do you mean when you say you're not there yet? Can you elaborate?"

Eli nods. "Yes. Our students told us we weren't ready. There was a subcommittee of the task force that was focused on student experiences. The subcommittee conducted research with a focus group of students, and they really wanted to hear about the students' experience at our institution. But the subcommittee had a really difficult time getting students to participate. I thought that was very telling. There wasn't this level of trust, either from students or even just students knowing what it's like to talk about their experiences. So when the research came back and was presented to the task force, it had three themes—feeling unwelcomed, feeling like they were not represented, and then the last one was feeling like there needed to be more diversity. The task force decided 'Oh, we're going to do presentations to other departments so that they're aware of these results.' Now, the task force is built out of different folks from the university. There's a few from marketing and admissions. We also have student development that's represented, and we have academic success and career development that's represented too. We took the presentations to each department and were able to share the research.

"It was a roadshow, sharing what HSI is and then sharing what we need to do to get there, but highlighting what we learned about the student experience. So I challenged departments and asked them, 'What are some ways we can change the students' experience?' A prominent quote from the research that came up was a senior student saying, 'I've never had a professor that looks like me or talks like me. I've never had a Latina professor.' As I was connecting with different departments, I asked them, 'What does your faculty look like? Are they ready to represent or serve Latino students? If they're not, what are you doing to help fix that?' In doing so, I've found that they're at different levels.

"The School of Education, they're very aware of it. They've developed a bilingual certificate for students that graduate and are able to get their teacher credential. So they work closely with the Spanish

Department, where a lot of Latinos end up majoring, or at least minoring in Spanish. So, yes, the School of Education is very in tune. They know the population. They know how to target or communicate with them. And then there are other departments where they're really struggling. The Psych Department—there's only one Latina professor there, and she's new. This is her first school year, so she's not even aware of these dynamics. So we're just not ready to serve Latino students across the university."

After a brief pause, I ask, "Have you changed any of your admissions practices in order to reach your HSI goal?"

"There was an increased focus on building transfer pathways," Eli says. "What the numbers showed was that the way Hispanic students were arriving to our institution was through being transfer students. It was concerning for me because those transfer pathways are not very strong. It's a broken system, but then our institution had some additional issues. Our registrar noticed we were promising new students a three-year graduation. But when the registrar did the math, she said there's no way. No transfer student is leaving in three years. They finish in three and a half, and depending on some majors, there're all these additional classes that some students don't account for. Yeah, the math wasn't adding up. So this year, again, the issue was a big thing with the board. They were able to decrease the number of units required to ensure a three-year graduation date, but that won't be implemented until the following school year. It's a big deal for the board to approve, but it was for the purpose of strengthening transfer. And then out of the HSI initiatives that I oversee, there was a transfer scholarship added. So, again, that's endowment money that is now being allotted for transfer students. There are feeder community colleges we're targeting more heavily, but again, we know the reality of transfer pathways, and it's really difficult, period. And then to add this level of extra hoops that students need to jump through, I'm like, 'Why would they come?' But there were a few other things we did. There have been incentives added, so if you live in certain counties, you get an additional $1,000. You come to visit the university your senior year, you get another $1,000. So we just added more incentives.

"Previously we had a multicultural outreach office. That was a function out of admissions. But that was dissolved. It had been active for over 30 years. They were the folks that would focus on doing active outreach. They always had a bilingual staff. They also had a group of students that would go out and visit different high schools. The students were the ones sharing about the university, and the students themselves were bilingual. We also used to focus on churches, but that was dissolved in 2020 with the hope that it wouldn't just be housed in the multicultural outreach office but that the responsibility would be shared by different counselors. But that didn't happen. Especially when COVID came and all the visits or the recruitment had to happen online, that went away. Now that we're back, at least when I started working, I noticed I kept getting pulled into the admissions space, and I was very quick to say 'No, that is not why I'm here. I'm not an admissions counselor. You can hire those. You have the budget to do that.' But I also noticed very quickly there is a vacuum there because the multicultural outreach office no longer exists, and there's a need to build that up. There's new leadership in place now, at least in admissions. We've had quite a lot of turnover in that space. So there is a need to revamp the admissions office, but as of right now, it hasn't been a priority. I believe the person that just started there, she has intentions to rehire a multicultural outreach person, but I don't know what that looks like right now. It is important."

I pause to take this all in. When I talked to Lily, she seemed excited about her job, while Eli seems a bit frustrated. I'm thinking about the complexities I want to convey in this story. "Is there anything else you'd like to add about your role and the HSI work you've been doing?"

"Honestly," Eli says, "my first year in this role was a lot of what I would call basics, laying down basics. So institutional membership with HACU, attending the AHSIE conference, connecting with Excelencia in Education. It really has been connecting the institution with folks that are already doing HSI work and that are experts in the field. As I mentioned, I work with the Division of Diversity and Inclusion, and I'm helping really to equip and educate our faculty and staff. Working with those teams connecting with students that are here already, as well as with the team that's trying to recruit new students. I keep voicing that this work cannot be done just in a silo, or it can't be just my office. So I'm sharing as much of the work as I can or challenging some of the other departments that get to participate in this work—because it lives in so many spaces. I think to be an HSI touches the university as a whole. I'm pushing everyone on campus—the financial aid counselors, the admissions team, the faculty. Especially the marketing team. I've told them all that if somebody calls—that's the very first step, then there's the application process and the financial aid process, which is a big one. The biggest lesson I've shared with them is that, when we talk about money, this is a family decision. If there isn't anyone informing families or walking them through this, the families are not going to feel confident. They're not going to feel like they can trust this institution. So that's been a big lesson I've shared with the financial aid team.

"I think the hard part is sharing that it's difficult work and sharing that it's not going to happen overnight. Just because you decided we're going to be an HSI, we can't make it happen overnight. It's difficult to share the data and say, 'No, we have patterns of not serving students well. We have low enrollment in this area' and to just be honest and say, 'This is the reality of our institution.' So as much as I appreciate the support and the authority that comes with having the institution's attention on this topic, it doesn't lessen the work that it requires."

I wait a moment, thinking about these issues, before thanking Eli for her time. "I appreciate you talking to me today. This has been really informative. I'll stop recording now and let you get back to your day. I'll let you know when the story will be published." Eli thanks me and says goodbye.

I have my final interview in an hour, so I grab my laptop and start writing again. I originally thought this story was going to be more celebratory, but I think I need to convey the complexities in the process of becoming an HSI. Lily and Eli have provided important perspectives on the accomplishments achieved and challenges faced as campuses seek the HSI designation. I really want to share these divergent perspectives and the tensions in becoming an HSI.

Moving Together and Adapting as a Collective

12:54 p.m. I have a few minutes before my next interview, so I make myself some coffee. I enjoy a few sips and settle in at my desk. Taylor has chosen to do the interview by phone, so I dial her number.

"Hello, this is Taylor. How can I help you?"

"Hi, Taylor, this is Nayeli. Thank you for taking my call. Is this still a good time to talk about being an HSI?"

"Yes, I can chat for a few minutes," Taylor says. "But it's been a hectic morning, and I might get pulled into a meeting soon."

"No problem, I'll keep it short, and if you need to get off, we can reschedule. Do you mind if I record our conversation?"

"No, not at all," she says.

"OK, great. Could you please start by telling me about the HSI efforts on your campus?"

"Sure. We were federally designated and recognized as an HSI before I got here. I've been on campus for almost eight years. We got the designation just a couple years before I arrived, but it's sort of, well, we got the designation, and nothing really was done with it or about it. It was just sort of 'Oh, yeah, we're an HSI.' I was hired as a diversity coordinator, and that was the only kind of DEI position we had on campus at the time. It was very much just student focused. There wasn't any sort of college-wide policy-type stuff happening around DEI or being an HSI. So when I took on that role, there was this idea that it was sort of, hey, just put on fun events for students, that sort of thing, and I advised the Latino/Chicano Club, which was awesome and amazing, but also very compartmentalized into just focusing on students, with no effort to innovate or change policy or the college. Slowly I started having those conversations and pushing and finding allies on campus. I have some really great allies in different areas, in our CAMP program, in our Chicano/Chicanx Studies program, and I just started building a group of us who are really focused on DEI and HSI.

"So with that, I pushed for a group to meet around the idea of 'How can we be an HSI? How can we be DEI-focused on campus?' Then that was kind of derailed because the college was setting up these core councils for shared governance—they wanted us to be enveloped into a core council around culture and diversity, which unfortunately really watered down the work that the group wanted to do and the real things we were excited to have happen. But some of us kept meeting and were still part of the core councils, and we collaborated on some pieces. Then my position was changed to be director of DEI for the college. That was seen as a little bit beyond just serving students. I was starting to get asked to come to more conversations, and we were starting to really have those conversations around what it means for us to be an HSI, and how we need to be talking about that and we need to be changing how we do things. So there started to be a bit more momentum."

I jump in. "So is there an HSI director or director of Hispanic initiatives?"

"No," Taylor says. "We haven't hired anyone to specifically oversee HSI work, or even initiatives for Latine students, despite enrolling 45% Latine students. Most of our HSI efforts emerged through this small group of dedicated people, with no area solely taking on the HSI work. For example, we worked really hard to get a diversity requirement passed for graduation. One of the things we worked on through the core council—but it had originally come from that group of really committed people on campus—is having this diversity requirement for graduation. I think that's been a big piece of exposing all our students to different perspectives. Really, it was interesting at the time—the Chicano/Chicanx Studies professor was saying most of the students who take his classes are Latinx. That's who takes his classes. It was this funny thing of, like, it would be great if our white students were also coming and learning this, and our other diverse students were coming and learning some of this. But those classes were seen as just for Latinx students. So with the diversity requirement, courses like that have been taken by a much broader array of students, which I think has been really great.

"So, yeah, this small group of people on campus has been leading a lot of the HSI efforts without the leadership of a director. And we've mostly been going to different conferences and talking to colleagues and realizing, oh, we're an HSI, but we don't make anything of that designation. We just say it or claim it, but it's not changing the way we're doing anything. And so that push and momentum around conversations, and honestly I think around a lot of the Black Lives Matter movement—some of that really made race conversations on campus a lot more prevalent and a lot more like, 'Hey, how are we serving the students we have?' Our student body is about 45% Latinx, and I think for a long time, they were just served the same way as everyone else. There wasn't this idea that we should be doing things differently, other than very specifically in our CAMP—our College Assistance Migrant Program—and in our TRIO programs or other pocket areas. So it's been a slow conversation shift, and I think a lot of leadership deans specifically, but even the VPs, they've really tried to infuse HSI into conversations around leadership, like, 'How have you thought about this in the context of us being an HSI?' So kind of changing those conversations so people realize, oh, we need to be thinking about it through that lens when we're doing our work."

"OK, so this small group is driving a lot of change," I say. "Do you have any HSI grants for the work you do?"

"We don't," Taylor says. "We applied last year, and we weren't selected. But we were very close to being selected. So we're trying to get that funding. The grant would allow us to focus on curriculum redesign. The diversity requirement is good, but we haven't changed any of our curriculum along with that policy. And we only implemented that requirement for our students getting transfer degrees, so that means people working on general transfer degrees to four-year schools. Our hope is to embed the diversity requirement into more of our technical programs too, so our automotive students would also get exposed to this, and our nursing students would get exposed to this, and our pharmacy tech students, and so on. So that's another piece of that—trying to integrate that requirement within the technical programs."

"Can you say a little more about the curriculum redesign?"

"Yes. With our Title V grant application, we were really trying to work on culturally responsive pedagogy and specifically creating support for faculty who want to innovate and change. One of the things we've recognized is that there are a lot of faculty who are excited and want to do things differently, but they don't know how or don't understand how to change what they've been doing for a long time. So yeah, we are really trying to get curriculum, culturally responsive pedagogy coach-type positions on our instruction side to help faculty who want to innovate. One of the things we have come to realize on our campus is that it's really difficult to require something of everyone, and not everyone is going to get on board, but if we can find those champions who want to innovate, then we can help them in their courses to do that, and then it becomes a model for other faculty to look at. We're also conducting an equity audit that we hope can show some of those areas where our diverse students may not be succeeding in certain courses, and we're going to try to pinpoint that a little more, which is scary for faculty. So we need to look at the issues more from a perspective of what's being done differently in these courses versus those courses, instead of trying to call out individuals. But yeah, there's movement around how we can help our diverse students be more successful in certain courses, the courses where we can look at the data and say that, right now, our diverse students are not as successful."

"Thank you for expanding," I say. "What other things has your campus done to serve such a large percentage of Latinx students?"

"There's been a big push for increasing our staff diversity. That's one thing we've had a big change in, which can really be seen over the last 8 to 10 years. Not so much in faculty. We've still really struggled with that, and I'd say we probably haven't changed much there. We add diverse faculty positions, and then they leave. So it doesn't feel like we've actually moved the needle with faculty. But with staff, we definitely have improved. We have a lot of bilingual-bicultural staff now, and that's been really exciting to see. I think our students connect in a very different way with our diverse staff across campus, which is exciting.

"We were also able to add another counselor on our campus recently. So now we have three full-time counselors. Two of them are

Spanish speaking, Latinx. I think I've really seen a difference in how they connect to students and just provide services in a really different way. Actually, we also added a position that's like a scheduler coordinator, and that person is also bilingual-bicultural. So I've really seen the counseling department grow and open in a different way. And I think our students are getting support in a different way. I've seen—like, a lot of times with student government members who are struggling—that I can walk them over to a counselor who they can really connect with, and they can speak in either language. I've seen it change the way they're getting services provided too. So that's been an exciting change. There's also been a push to create community and culture through the counseling department. They just did a wellness event for staff that was really exciting and had a lot of cultural pieces. And same thing with students. The counseling department offers wellness sessions students can drop in on. Instead of the sessions being individual meetings with students, they're much broader and just more inclusive of different ways of being.

"We also hired more bilingual-bicultural outreach and admissions staff. In the past, we always had recruiters who didn't speak Spanish, who were not Latinx. But our three most-recent recruiters have all been fluent in Spanish and identify as Latinx themselves. So that shift in who's out in the community representing our college and talking to prospective students, talking to the community, building those partnerships has really changed because our staff makeup has changed, and we've prioritized being fluent in Spanish. It used to not be a requirement for a recruiter, and now it is. That's definitely changed how we connect with the community.

"We also made sure that when being bilingual is a requirement of the job, then staff do get a pay differential for it. Unfortunately, for a lot of our jobs, bilingualism is still just preferred and not required. So when it's preferred and staff do speak Spanish, they don't get paid extra. That's a fight I'm still trying to win. But yeah, if it's required, they do get paid differentially. And despite some changes, there is still a huge burden on our Spanish-speaking staff, those of us who do get constantly pulled into other things that are not part of our jobs because a Spanish speaker is needed. It is definitely still a fight and still just assumed that skill can be used by whoever wants to use it. But the nice thing is that, because our staff has become so much more diverse—I mean, on my team over half of us, probably three-quarters of us speak Spanish fluently. So at least the extra work is spread out a bit more. The situation has changed, and it's not all on one person, so it's not like, 'Oh, go to that one person.' It's like, 'No, many, many of us speak Spanish.' Sorry, I got lost, what was the question again?"

"No problem," I say. "I asked what other things your campus has done to serve Latinx students?"

"Right. We've also done a lot of trainings, and kind of changed the narrative, where we're talking about being an HSI and trying to infuse it into the work we do in many different areas. Some of that has involved changing the physical space on campus and having murals that are reflective of diverse people and really trying to have it feel like, when you walk onto campus, you're at an HSI. Even some of the music we play in our student lounge every day—we play very diverse music, and people feel that it just feels different—not everywhere on campus but in certain spaces. We're not fully there yet, but we have pockets of feeling that sense of belonging and students seeing themselves reflected in staff across campus.

"Oh, and I haven't mentioned that for graduation, one of the things we've done is we now offer our whole graduation ceremony in Spanish and in English. We translate the entire thing. It's also a public event, and it's streamed live. The first year we did that, people were all up in arms about it—'It's so long, and it's so this, and it's so whatever.' But we've normalized it over the last three or four years. Just to see people's families there, and they're able to fully understand everything and be present in it—I feel that for a lot of our Latinx students to have their language and culture represented in that moment is so important to them and to their family. It's been really important. And yes, the ceremony is long. We do try to pretranslate everything, so the interpreter does have it kind of scripted out, and they're not having to do everything. We do bigger chunks at a time. But yeah, it does take longer, and we had to cut out some other things in order to accommodate two languages, but the impact is huge. It makes a big difference for students, hearing it all in both languages. To me, it feels like a very public display of 'We are an HSI, and we're trying to do dual languages and trying to really represent who our students are.'

"The last thing I'll mention before I have to jump off—I'm being called into a meeting—is that when I started my position and started working with that small group of dedicated people—changemakers, if you will—we were not as focused on policy and structural changes. We were focused on student-facing efforts, but we've moved toward more substantial policy work. We now have a DEI strategic plan for our campus, which was a big moment and a big change for us. The funny thing is it's now a requirement for the state, and we didn't work on it until it was an actual requirement for us, but I'm still very proud of it. The group of people who sat down and worked on creating the document. We're very diverse but also very focused on being an HSI and how we can make sure those voices are uplifted and how to keep that as the focus.

"One of the things we're really proud of in that document is the vision statement, which specifically calls out Latinx and Indigenous students and community. Part of that came from reading Dr. Gina Garcia's work and having that conversation about why we need to call out who we're focusing on in our mission and vision. But honestly, that created a lot of pushback and a lot of drama from people who thought we were leaving everyone else out. I actually had to stand down our board of trustees about that vision statement. I basically got told we were being discriminatory for calling that out in our vision statement. Ultimately, they ended up approving the plan and passing it, and it is in place for the college, which was a huge win for the group that was so excited about the new vision. To me, the plan is very much a real living document we can now look to and say, 'This is how we're HSI-focused, and this is what we're looking at.' And we cannot have it be—I mean, most of the time I've worked here, there has been very fluffy language around 'all students and diverse students' and expressing just very broad, general things. People aren't usually willing to actually call something out and say 'We're going to do this for this group of people.' So I'm really proud that it's changing the way we're thinking about the work," Taylor says.

I feel a deep sense of joy listening to her, knowing there is a lot of intentional work going on in some colleges and universities to serve Latine students. "Thank you for sharing a few minutes of your day with me, Taylor," I say. "I know you're busy, and I appreciate your time. I'll let you know when the story is published."

Theorizing the Processes of Servingness

Thursday morning. I've had time to really think about this article. I'm most intrigued by the intentionality, time, and effort going into the HSI work at some campuses, and I want to provide a space for that in this story. My editor gave me some autonomy with it, so I'm going to write about the process, porque el proceso es bonito.[1] One thing I learned from my interviews is that the process of becoming an HSI really is beautiful—it's a process to be embraced yet not rushed. As I think about how I want to write about this, I separate the tasks and activities from the processes (see table 3.1 on the next page).

Creating this list is helping me envision the various processes as planning, learning, exploration, collaboration, leadership, and implementation. There might be other ways to think about this, but I'm satisfied with the list for now. I'll come back to it after lunch. I close my laptop to take a break. It's time to step outside and enjoy this sunny day in Chicago.

1. This statement is inspired by a news article by Waubonsee Community College, an HSI in Illinois. Waubonsee Community College. (2021, July 15). *El proceso es bonito: Waubonsee Community College helps Latinx students realize "beauty in the process."* Waubonsee Community College News & Events. https://www.waubonsee.edu/news-events/news/el-proceso-es-bonito-waubonsee-community-college-helps-latinx-students-realize-beauty-process

Table 3.1
Identifying the Processes of Servingness

Tasks and Activities	Processes of Servingness
Launch an HSI planning committee.	Planning
Conduct a SWOT analysis.	Planning
Include HSI in the campus strategic plan.	Planning
Do research with students (e.g., focus groups).	Planning
Create Latine-focused outreach, recruitment, and admissions practices.	Implementation
Hire bilingual and bicultural outreach, admissions, and financial aid staff.	Implementation
Hire bilingual and bicultural counseling and advising staff.	Implementation
Implement an HSI cluster hire for faculty.	Implementation
Change hiring practices.	Implementation
Change the curriculum to be antiracist, equity-centered, and Latine-focused.	Implementation
Create diversity requirements for graduation.	Implementation
Build relationships with campus partners (e.g., student affairs, admissions, faculty).	Collaboration
Build relationships with community organizations.	Collaboration
Work with alumni engagement staff and Latine alumni.	Collaboration
Train faculty and staff to serve Latine students.	Learning
Train faculty and staff to identify and disrupt racism and microaggressions.	Learning
Hire an HSI director.	Leadership
Collaborate with marketing and communications.	Communication
Change the HSI narrative.	Communication
Launch an HSI website.	Communication
Present HSI inquiry findings to the campus.	Communication

4

Leading for Change from the Middle

. . . the desire for a society where there is more interdependence—
mutual reliance and shared leadership, vision.
—adrienne maree brown, *Emergent Strategy: Shaping Change, Changing Worlds* (2017)

STRONG LEADERSHIP IS NEEDED FOR TRUE transformation at HSIs. HSIs need leaders with vision who can enact organizational change and advance a Latine-serving identity. They need leaders who can see the bigger picture of what the campus could be as an HSI—beyond enrollment, eligibility, and grant seeking—not leaders who simply implement HSI grants, spend the money, and report to the federal government, which keeps the campus in a Latine-enrolling status. Following the defunding of HSI grants in September 2025, visionary leadership is crucial. HSI leaders come in many forms, including those in senior-level administrative roles (presidents, vice presidents, chancellors, provosts), as well as mid-level leaders (deans, directors, chairs) and grassroots leaders who may not hold positional titles but who lead from the bottom and middle of the organization (faculty, student services coordinators) (Kezar & Lester, 2011). HSI leaders are sometimes Title V or Title III grant directors but not always, and some campuses have moved toward hiring an official HSI director to oversee all HSI activities, regardless of HSI eligibility or grant getting (Garcia, 2022, November 7; Garcia, 2024, January 28; Garcia, 2024, October 6). There are many leaders on campus who take on the HSI work, sometimes for personal reasons because they are self-identified Latines who care deeply about Latine students and other times because it is in their job description or because they were asked by senior leaders to guide the HSI efforts.

One type of HSI leader is known as an "institutional agent." Institutional agents are educators who have access to social capital, campus resources, and extensive networks and who actively work to pass these forms of capital on to minoritized students (Stanton-Salazar, 2011). Garcia and Ramirez (2018) found that institutional agents at one HSI directly supported Latine students by creating on-campus jobs or funding them to attend conferences. Other institutional agents served as advocates for Latine students at a systemic level, questioning campus policies that harm students and calling attention to inequitable outcomes and experiences. Most importantly, institutional agents challenged systems of oppression, highlighted racialized injustices, and sought to dismantle structures and practices that create inequities (Garcia & Ramirez, 2018). Bensimon et al. (2019) similarly found that STEM faculty at two HSIs served as institutional agents by challenging normative notions of excellence and elevating the unique potential and cultural characteristics that Latine students brought to campus. Some worked at the individual level, creating direct opportunities for Latine students to participate in labs and research opportunities, while others worked at the systemic level, changing policies and articulation agreements to enhance successful transfer from community colleges into four-year institutions.

An important characteristic of institutional agents is that they are often high-status leaders on campus who possess positional power. Alternatively, grassroots leaders are those who do not have formal authority within the organization but who create change from the bottom up (Meyerson, 2001). Grassroots leaders are activists within the institution who seek to change the organization from within, often forming coalitions with other changemakers. Yet they require a unique set of skills and resilience as they often face barriers and challenges when they try to disrupt the organizational status quo (Kezar, 2010). Quinteros and Covarrubias (2023) documented the way faculty of color who were grassroots leaders at one HSI navigated structural barriers while enacting change. They found that faculty of color took on invisible labor because of the high enrollment of students of color who sought them out for mentorship and guidance, yet the institution provided limited resources for the faculty. Instead these grassroots leaders sought out funding to equip themselves with the resources they needed to support students. They often worked through informal networks to enact change rather than relying on formal top-down systems that they suggested moved too slowly.

Similarly, Nuñez (2022) found that faculty in computer science departments at four HSIs led efforts to change the culture of servingness within their departments with a focus on developing race-conscious and equity-minded environments. They did this by emphasizing a talent-development mindset that centered students' potential for success rather than their performance on normative metrics. Faculty also stressed a shared vision of student success that emphasized good teaching practices and the recruitment of new faculty who were committed to teaching through a culturally relevant approach. Poza et al. (2022) documented the movidas made by Latine mid-level leaders at one HSI that helped to disrupt the deficit narrative about Latine students on campus. These movidas included building strategic relationships on campus, influencing policies by working with key administrators on campus, and expanding roles on campus that have a heavy influence on Latine students. Leaders at HSIs also empower student leaders, with educators like Arlene Cano Matute (formerly at the University of California, Riverside) engaging students in HSI participatory action research (Garcia, 2023, September 24) and Desiree (Dez) Zuniga at Pasadena City College hiring students to advance student-level servingness (Garcia, 2023, October 22). These leadership processes are crucial to true transformation for HSIs.

High-level administrators also advance a servingness agenda, with a growing body of research highlighting the role of presidents and vice presidents in these efforts. Ponjuan et al. (2017) interviewed six HSI community college presidents to understand how they influenced organizational change and found that, despite active resistance and skepticism toward serving Latine students, these presidents became unapologetic in their efforts to serve while actively shaping the campus HSI narrative. They also used disaggregated data that showed inequities by race-ethnicity and gender to create dissonance about the disconnect between a commitment to serving and the actual success of Latine students. McNaughtan and Lujan (2023) similarly asked five HSI community college presidents about their role in enacting servingness. These presidents stressed they actively increased representation of Latine faculty and administrators and prepared future leaders of color for the institution. They also provided opportunities for robust training and critical dialogue on campus and sought resources to ensure success of Latine students. Strong high-level administrators also empower others on campus to do HSI work. For example, Marla Franco at the University of Arizona created an HSI fellowship program for faculty and staff on campus to learn about HSI concepts and implement their own HSI projects (Garcia, 2022, November 7), while Manuel Del Real at Metropolitan State University of Denver launched the Hanover Grants Academy to provide guidance and training for the pursuit of competitive grants that support institutional advancement (Garcia, 2024, January 28).

In this chapter, I focus on leadership and argue that all types of leaders at HSIs matter—meaning, high-level administrators who model servingness and shape HSI narratives, mid-level leaders who use their decision-making power to enact servingness, and grassroots leaders who lead in community from the lower levels of the organization. Grassroots leaders align closely with the emergent strategy framework as they often start social movements within the organization. Yet emergent strategy calls for interdependent relationship building where leaders can rely on one another to work toward the collective good (brown, 2017). Both the servingness framework and the transforming HSIs framework highlight leadership as an essential dimension of servingness, calling attention to the decision-making that addresses policies, practices, and procedures that center the lived realities and equitable outcomes and experiences of Latine students. There are multiple approaches to leadership worth considering in the organizational change efforts at HSIs, but emergent strategy centers grassroots leadership and the small, incremental changes that drive bigger transformation. Emergent strategy also stresses collaborative action, accountability, and vulnerable leadership (brown, 2017). As such, this chapter focuses on this type of leadership.

Leading from the Middle

This counterstory is about grassroots leaders who drive HSI work from the middle—not from the highest levels of administration. HSI change efforts often start from the ground up, and change agents can come from any part of the organization. The counterstory here brings to life the realities of mid-level leaders trying to change HSIs, and it highlights both the wins and the challenges. Resilience is necessary in the fight to dismantle structures that are not serving Latine students, and grassroots leaders often face adversity. Yet they must remain hopeful in the face of a nonlinear process that offers successes and setbacks in the push to become a Latine-serving campus.

Our narrator is Connie, an HSI community college leader who serves as dean of equity. In this role, she oversees a variety of initiatives on campus, including the campus intercultural center, which was designed as a support space for students of color, veterans, undocumented students, and LGBTQIA+ students. Connie is a positional leader on campus with a vision for creating a campus environment that values the community cultural wealth of diverse students. But she feels alone in some of her efforts to advance an HSI agenda. Despite having support from upper administration to advance equity efforts, she doesn't have collective buy-in from faculty and staff to elevate the campus's HSI identity. She is frustrated because the campus is not committed to being an HSI despite achieving HSI enrollment and eligibility for over 20 years, as well as receiving multiple Title V grants. Every time she tries to elevate HSI conversations, she is met with resistance.

Connie is meeting with two friends from graduate school who are also mid-level administrators at HSIs. Daniel works at an HSI community college and has extensive experience leading Title V and Title III grants on his campus. Esperanza works at a four-year HSI and serves as HSI director. She's visiting from out of state for a conference, so now is the perfect chance for the three of them to have a reunion. Since they haven't seen each other in several years, they're meeting for cafecito to catch up on work as well as life. Connie's growing concerns about the HSI efforts on her campus are on her mind, and she plans to seek support from her friends, who, in her opinion, are some of the strongest HSI leaders in the field.

Cafecito and Chisme

I pull into the parking garage blasting Caifanes (yes, I'm that girl), and the song finishes as I find a spot for my electric vehicle. I change out of my snakeskin heels, which gave boss-lady vibes all day, into my cheetah-print flats, which give tired-millennial-mami-after-a-long-day vibes. I'm ready to relax and see my amigues. I walk into the coffee shop and smell the fresh aroma of café, which always brings a smile to my face. I see Daniel sitting at a table near the back where we can have some privacy—you never know who could walk in cuando estamos chismeando. I wave at Daniel as he gets up to greet me.

"Hola Connie, ¿cómo estás?"

"Muy bien, how are you?"

"Aqui nomás. ¿Quieres algo?"

"Yes, but I've never been to this place—let me see what they have. Y Esperanza?"

"No sé."

"OK, I'll text her."

We walk over to the counter to order our coffee. We talk, catching up on life, family, kids, and all that good stuff. I've known Daniel for a long time, but we don't see each other often, so we always have a lot to catch up on. As we order, I see Esperanza from the corner of my eye.

She runs over, hugs us, and screams, "Oh, I've missed you both so much!"

The Status Quo Won't Save Us

We all talk for a few minutes while we wait for our coffee and then walk back to our table. As we sit down, I cut to the chase. "Oye, I need some advice."

"Cuéntanos," Daniel says.

"I'm so frustrated with the HSI efforts on my campus." I shake my head. "Every time I feel like we're making any progress, something happens that reminds me this is all performative. I just feel like we've made a lot of progress toward equity but not toward HSI. And I know they're related in many ways, but it feels like people don't really care about our Latine students because they represent 50% of our student population. We've always had the HSI designation, but we really don't know what that means, and we aren't really doing anything targeted for Latine students. But I think, if you're going to be an HSI, you need to be doing something targeted and specific for Latino or Hispanic students.

"So our student equity efforts have really overshadowed the HSI work because of the state mandate to implement equity plans." I'm really getting into it now. "We're calling out identity markers and then creating initiatives that address the issues of that identity group. But as you know, the state asked us to look at more than just Latino and Hispanic students, so it's almost like the equity planning process has drowned out any efforts to think about equity for our largest population. My colleagues basically want to do something for all students. A lot of them say, 'Oh, well, we're already an HSI, and we already have HSI grants, we're already serving Latino students.' And I'm like, 'No, Latine students need additional support. Let's talk about Tara Yosso's work on community cultural wealth, let's talk about the role of our students' cultural capital, let's help them see the cultural capital they bring to the institution, and let's do programming around that, having those discussions. And maybe let's bring in their families because their families, to them, to us, they're vital and key. So let's not just say that we're applying for HSI funding and that we get the funding because of the population we naturally serve geographically. Let's do something intentional.

"And really, what came first, the chicken or egg? The equity conversation is more recent and state mandated, but we've been an HSI for over 20 years. We really were an HSI first, before we became equity-minded. And so I've realized I'm doing all this equity work, which is great because the state is forcing me to do it and they can't tell me no, right? I'm like, I have to do it. The state is telling me to. So I've got the state, I've got the president, I've got the VP. We've got people who are saying that you have to do this work. Good. I understand the intentionality behind the work and the targeted nature of the efforts so they'll hopefully be successful. I get that. But folks aren't seeing the HSI component—the Latine component, the Hispanic-serving component of the equity work I'm leading—which for me is probably the hardest because we have such a big population. Historically, we've received grants time and time again. Pretty much we just applied for them, and we knew we were going to get some kind of federal funding because of our population. But we weren't doing anything intentional for Latino students. And unfortunately, that's the challenge. I hate to put it this way, but there is the pitting of, well, 'Why are we doing something for Latino students that's intentional when there's so many of them? We don't have an equity gap for Latino students because there's so many.' And I'm like, 'But there are equity gaps for our Latine students, not necessarily in enrollment but in outcomes.'

"And often it is some of the other marginalized groups who say, 'Well, we have few people of this population, so we need to do more to attract more and to support them.' Yes, we do need to do more to increase our numbers and to support them through the pathways. Yes, we do. But what's the benefit of saying that, because we have a large number of Latinos and we get HSI funding every time we apply for it, we shouldn't do anything more intentional? I feel like we're doing intentional work here for our Black students, for our LGBTQIA+ students, for our veteran students—we're doing intentional work here because that's how we're going to help that population succeed.

But we also need to do intentional work with our Latine population. And this is not the Olympics of who's more marginalized—I don't want to play that game." I shake my head again.

"I mean, by default we have these populations in our institution. Geographically, this is where we are. We're in a place where there's a lot of Latinos. So as a community college serving the community surrounding us, we're going to have a lot of Latinos here. But we're not doing anything intentional. And if you look at our HSI programming, you wouldn't know it was HSI programming because it's open to everyone. There isn't any conversation about why you're in this program. There isn't anything about how you're special, you're talented, you bring this unique cultural perspective to the work, so use it, thrive, uplift yourself, uplift your community. None of that. So I'm like, this might as well be any other generic program on campus. I think if we're doing equity work, it needs to happen with our HSI efforts too. But it isn't happening, and I can't seem to convince people we should focus on Latino students." I pause, realizing I haven't taken a breath in quite a while.

Daniel nods thoughtfully. "Oye," he says. "We have the same desmadres on my campus. One of our counselors who was hired under the Title V grant to work with transfer students was recently moved to the campus Transfer Center. We could say that's a win, as the position is getting institutionalized. Pero I'm not sure it is a win because now that they've been transferred, they have a different role. Under Title V, they focused on Latine students, but that will now be expanded. Yes, they can have a bigger impact, but my colleagues keep saying, 'Oh, now they're going to serve everybody.' Pero I don't want them to serve everybody. By serving everybody they serve nobody. I need to make sure they have a more specific focus, where they're able to support a certain group of students that I know for a fact is going to be targeted—I know for a fact it's going to be communicated—and that group is Latinos.

"One of the sayings I hate the most—and I will use that word because I do hate it—is 'Rising tides lift all boats,' or algo asi. It gets thrown around all the time, but I don't agree. Just think back to our equity-mindedness. That saying is about keeping the status quo. It's not going to raise everything equitably. Those that are already high are going to stay there. And those that are lower are going to stay lower even though everything is going up. It doesn't work for me. I mean, if you have a yacht, your yacht rises too. But we have a lot of students with rowboats, and when the tide rises, those students still have just a rowboat, and they're never going to have a yacht unless we do something different. But when I raise those issues, I'm read as being challenging as opposed to wanting to actually serve our students the way we're supposed to as an equity-minded HSI."

I nod enthusiastically. "I hate that cliché too. It keeps the status quo and makes people feel like we're serving everyone well, but we're not. And I get it—we need to serve all our students. But when you disaggregate the data, our Latine students are struggling. I feel like the state mandates to address equity have us doing equity work the way we interpret it, but my campus doesn't think we have an equity issue for Latine students. It's really frustrating."

Leading Through Collaborative Action

Daniel and Esperanza commiserate with me for a while, just like they've often done over the years when I've shared my struggles. They've always been such good friends, and I'm so grateful. I finish my café and start to think more on the bright side.

"I don't want to be a complete downer," I say, "because there are great initiatives at the state and system level to support our equity work. The system has really been intentional about scaffolding initiatives, from the matriculation initiative to the equity initiative to the guided pathways initiative. And there is another mandate where all the colleges need to align their different funding sources to be leveraged to close equity gaps, to have students meet these metrics of access, persistence, completion, and transfer on a pathway to a career. If you have a very innovative college where all the parts work well together, then yes, it can work. But you have to have different budget managers—it could be a dean, it could be a VP—you just have to have budget managers stacking the dollars, leveraging them, and doing the work together to get from point A of access to point Z of exit and successful job placement or successful transfer. That's when it works. If we got to that point, we'd be doing really well. And that's the scaffolded approach the system chancellor had in terms of how these initiatives were rolled out over a 7- to 10-year period. We're now seeing that approach happen a little bit more, and I think if we do it right, we could leverage the dollars to serve.

"Along those lines, I was able to do some collaborative work for the intercultural center. You see, we had parenting students that were Latino or Black, and I was supporting them in the equity efforts in the center because they identified as either Latino or Black and they were part of the programs I had. Well, as parenting students, they could benefit from other dollars and other programs, but I didn't oversee those budgets. So I had to work closely with my deans who oversaw those budgets to figure out how we could support this parenting student with your dollars and my dollars together. Because, again, the goal is to get the student to transfer or to get the student whatever career they're intending to achieve. So I think that goes back to the people in the organization—we need to put our egos aside and not just say 'Oh, my dollars are serving my people.' But say, like, 'How can your dollars and my dollars work together to more holistically serve the student?' Because you win and I win if we're talking about the metrics that we have to report on and accountability. But ultimately the student wins because they're on a career path. And that should be everyone's goal, right? I don't care about you winning and me winning—the student wins, which is really what should be driving us all."

Daniel jumps in. "Exactly! You have to be strategic about how initiatives work together. And you can do that with HSI grants too. It doesn't sound like your campus sees it that way, but my campus does. Our current Title V grant that I oversee extends the guided pathways work we started with state funding, and it really focuses on the courses that are, como se dice, gateway courses. So it really focuses, or rather changes, some of the curriculum to develop some of the liberatory outcomes that Dr. Garcia talks about—really focusing on that work through the actual curriculum. Our grant director was very strategic and very specific in embedding the guided pathways' framework word by word into our actual grant. It was designed to help that, pero one of the issues for me—and this is one I always work on with my team—it's asking the question, well, what is the tangible component that's actually addressing our Latinx population? And those are the attainment goals or the objectives that I always emphasize too. We said we were going to serve our Latinx students, but how are we doing that? I'm looking to really hold us accountable to discuss the guided pathways model through the lens of servingness and Latinx success. I literally hold up the *Becoming Hispanic-Serving Institutions* book and show them the chart in chapter 2."

"Wait you know the actual chapter in the book?" Esperanza exclaims.

Daniel smiles. "Sí claro, don't you?"

We all laugh. I shrug my shoulders. "I mean, yeah, I guess I do."

"Yeah, of course," Daniel says. "I have to hold my people on campus accountable for serving Latinx students, so I use the book all the time. I turn to the page, and I even have one of those little sticky notes to mark the page—" we all laugh again "—y entonces les pregunto 'Well, what do you mean by HSI? How can we actually do servingness? And how can we proactively change the academic outcomes for Latinx students?' Luckily our previous Title V project director got it and worked through a Latina lens. She's also an academic, so she brought the HSI research to us. She's the one who assigned us the book. And that's when we had to grapple with some tough questions. What does it mean to be an HSI? What is my role in this Title V grant? And you know, some people didn't like that we were assigned a book. They thought it was slowing us down. No one ever said so explicitly, but those were the vibes. But the project director was like, 'Let's pause and create some frameworks. Let's identify what our mission is here and really align the goals of the grant.' I will say previous grants didn't have that. Most of the Title V directors would just pull people together and give them stipends. But they never offered clear guidance on what it means to be an HSI and what the goals of those specific Title V grants were. So the book gave us guidance on how we should approach this work. But we have to keep reminding people this is Title V and we're going to center Latinx students.

"We also need to make the connections between state-funded and federally funded initiatives—they are very much connected, and I think that's why we thrive in some areas. I'm involved in a lot of that funding tambien, and I'm part of various committees. I know the federal regulations, and I know the state regulations. State regulations allow for some stuff, federal ones don't, so it's really balancing out which one I could use to advance our efforts. For our programming, depending on what's going to be embedded, or what the goal is, if we're not really fully budgeted for X event, then I use the other funds to pay for it. So I'm constantly moving between different state and federal initiatives to make things happen. I am, in another life, probably an accountant—I really do love working with my numbers, so it's easy for me to show how we're using different funds, both state and federal. And I have a really good working relationship the HSI program officer in Washington, so I reach out with questions all the time."

I nod. "We've done some of that too. Because of the equity work that we do, it's not a fund source that covers everything. We've had to partner with different funding sources across the campus to expand the work we do. We partnered with our workforce dollars, and those monies were able to help us get to our disproportionately impacted parenting students because workforce dollars often support parenting students. So we leverage those to work together. And then we also partnered with our STEM NSF HSI funding because that grant was targeting Latinos pursuing STEM fields. So we leveraged the momentum we had from the last seven years to partner with different groups on campus that had different funding sources to strengthen the work we were doing and to make it more robust and more institutional because, again, one funding source can't do everything for everyone. So, yeah, like I said, we're doing good work, making a lot of progress to support minoritized students, but I just get frustrated because it's not usually Latine- or HSI-focused."

"Maybe you need to show them page 31 of *Becoming HSIs*," Esperanza says, and we all laugh loudly. "I'm joking," Esperanza says, "but on our campus we give out Dr. Garcia's book like it's candy."

Daniel slaps the table. "Eso! La madrina o que, la reina de HSIs!"

"Yeah, well, I brought Dr. Garcia to campus," I say, "and they still question me when I try to hold us accountable to HSI. I mean, it was good for some folks, and some of those folks are amazing people leading the equity efforts on campus, and they're the ones trying to convince the masses. We do have some really good people for whom her message was well received. And I brought in some other scholars from San Diego and USC, and they've been in a partnership with our district for two years now. When we bring these scholars into the room, it starts clicking for more people, so it matters. I know so many amazing scholars doing great work, and I learn from them all the time.

"And honestly," I continue, "my campus is pretty progressive. Our president is a queer woman. Our VP is a Latino man. And then there's me as a Latina woman serving as a dean. They trusted me with this role five years ago, knowing I could implement policy and design new policy and even change some of the structures, which for me was part of the challenge. When I bring forward ideas for institutional change, they're supportive of creating new programs that will become institutionalized. So I do think the leaders at my institution matter too. But there are some differences by generation. Some of the people in leadership, whether it be in the classroom or leading the institution, still kind of live by the status quo. And when I look at my peers who are doing equity-minded work and HSI work and intentional work, I feel like they're my generation. So the old guard is still doing things the way they did them before, and this new generation of leaders around my age-ish, us millennials, that's who's leading right now. Yeah, we're the ones that are like, no, we got to be intentional, and we have to learn from research, and we have to redesign the curriculum, and we must change the institution and be equity-minded."

Esperanza jumps in. "Oh, that's an interesting theory. So what you're saying is the older generations are stuck in their ways, and us younger millennials are more innovative and committed to equity and justice? And we do TikToks. I like it."

"Hold up," Daniel says. "I'm a Gen X, and I'm committed to this work too. So who are we talking about? Cómo se dice, baby boomers?"

We all laugh. Esperanza says, "Basically. And old Gen Xers, not you, eres joven. You're one of those Xlennials." More laughter.

Institutional Commitment Not Individual Rock Stars

"Mira, regardless of our generation, we are the new generation of leaders," Daniel says, bringing us back to the real conversation. "And I agree, the old guard doesn't like change. Pero I don't care. I understand policy, I understand budgets, I understand how state and federal dollars can be used to leverage servingness, and that's what I'm gonna do. My campus does equity work and HSI work, but we haven't had a collective movement, and we don't have an identified HSI leader. I've been doing HSI for a lot of years, so oftentimes I'm deemed the unofficial HSI person, and at times that can feel daunting. When there are HSI-related issues, my president will say things like 'Oh, I thought you had that handled.' I'm like, 'I have a job.' Sometimes I really struggle. Each HSI grant has a committee, a faculty lead, and an activities director. We meet to go over our grant objectives and make sure we're meeting them. But ultimately, there is no cohesion across our HSI grants. Or even what you're talking about, Connie—there is no cohesion across equity efforts. Everyone does their own thing and doesn't talk, which is a missed opportunity for elevating our efforts. Tengo muchos años doing HSI, and I have a lot of the knowledge, a lot of experience with the processes that go with it—what is allowed, what isn't allowed, and, more importantly, how you sell it. But I haven't been appointed as the official HSI director, so I can't be held accountable for what everyone is doing."

I nod again. "Yeah, I feel that. I'm the dean of equity, not the dean of HSI, so it's almost like people want me to do only equity work, not HSI work, which is ridiculous, because they go hand and hand. But maybe we need Esperanza to tell us about how she does this work since she *is* the dean of HSI."

Esperanza smiles with excitement. "Oh, I like that. I'm gonna ask for a title change." She puts her hands in the air and traces a frame as she says, "Dean of HSIs." She puts her hands down. "That sounds way more official than 'HSI director.'" We all laugh, and she continues. "Listen, just because you have an HSI director does not mean you have arrived as an HSI. It just means you're on your way and the campus is committed to that. We still have plenty of work to do. But I will say that I don't get the same sort of resistance from my colleagues that you're getting, Connie. So I appreciate that. But my office is small—only two full-time people including me, plus two student workers. So we obviously can't and shouldn't do all the work. We really see our role as relationship building. We spend a lot of time meeting with folks across campus, helping them understand what it means for our institution to be an HSI and then brainstorming with them and helping them lift things up or put things out there for students. And then we back off and say, 'Great, we've helped you, almost consulted with you.' And we let them really take the lead so we can then dive into other areas that maybe aren't doing the work or maybe are a little bit hesitant to do some of the HSI work we think we should be doing as a campus.

"We also do a lot of community building—we really get out in the community, locally and across various regions in the state. We have a lot of meetings with folks from the mayor's office, our congresspeople, different nonprofits across the state, and we engage with them and try to figure out how we can serve the students in our backyard, the ones that are kind of near us, really. I think logistically it's a lot of meetings. It's a lot of talking with folks and getting them to understand what it means for us to be an HSI. I think there's still a lot of work for us, in terms of how folks don't always understand what it means. A lot of times, we have to talk about the definition the Department of Education has given us, and then we say, 'But that's not it.' We have to figure out what our HSI identity is. So a lot of the work is still telling folks what it means for us to be an HSI as we also try to figure out our HSI identity.

"The other thing I will say is that I'm in a state that's not necessarily HSI friendly. You both talk about equity mandates and equity plans and even your position, Connie, as dean of equity. I would love all that, but we don't have that support from the state or the board of regents, which we report to as a public institution. Half of those regents are appointed by our governor, who is super rightwing and conservative. Those are the folks who our president has to go to for everything. And so that makes it difficult for us, where the state government and the board of regents are not always supportive of what we're doing as an HSI, and they're very hesitant for us to make some of those changes. And sometimes we have to pull back on our strategies because we're pushing too hard, and they aren't ready. And at the end of the day, I'm the one supporting my family, my kids, my parents, my abuela, and I'm the one who has health care for all of us, and sometimes I just need to back off a little, just to make sure I still have a job. I think that's the really hard part. We believe in this work, and we believe in change, but we see our colleagues in other states losing their jobs because of anti-DEI legislation." Esperanza sighs.

"So, yeah, it may seem like we've arrived as an HSI," she continues, "but some of it is performative too, like you said, Connie. We have an HSI website, but even some of that feels performative. I mean, there is a student resources section, and there is a section for faculty and staff where they can find resources, or they can find community or build community. But some of that is really about exposure and proving that we're doing something. There's a whole section where we post things when we're in the news or we have articles written about us, or when we receive any grants related to our HSI designation. Some of that's just to keep our work out there so our campus will continue to fund our HSI efforts, because my office isn't grant funded. So we have to produce, or the funding could go away. And so the website is also a place for accountability, a place where we show we're doing things, like, 'Look at all our great work.'"

"At least you have a website," Daniel says. "I mean, we do too, pero it took us a long time. So y'all are moving a lot faster than us old-school Tia HSIs have moved. Pero I hadn't thought about the website as a source of accountability. We used to just tell people 'Hey, look what we're doing as an HSI,' but that didn't make us an

HSI. I would tell the president, 'HSI is nowhere on our actual page—we don't even have a website that says that.' Again, granted, we've been an HSI for almost two decades, but we finally—just last year—we finally got our website. And now we're starting to do a lot more promotion of the work. We finally made an HSI logo, and that literally has taken years of trying to do too. We've had HSI grants since they first started coming out—we've had them from the get-go. Pero hasta recently we finally got a logo and shirts that people are actually wearing. I was in a meeting today, and one of the staff was wearing their shirt, and that just filled me with joy and pride like, 'Exactly, people want the shirt.' Something simple has meant so much for people. I gave one to our president, and the folks are wearing them, and people—students specifically—they're like, 'That is awesome. Thank you for this, I didn't know we had so many Latinx students.'"

I jump in. "Well, damn, we're an old-school Tia HSI too, but we don't have a website or a logo or T-shirts or nada. This is why I get so frustrated. There is no pride in being an HSI the way it seems like there is on your campuses. Students don't even know we're an HSI. And there's no real desire to make that part of our identity, and I'm struggling with that. I'm struggling to make that pride our reality too, because I think if anyone should be making those efforts, it's me as the dean of equity, since we don't have an HSI director. But there's no intentional discussion on what it means to be Latino-serving or Hispanic-serving. And again, I keep going back to the cultural wealth conversation. How are we engaging with our Latine students' community, their culture, their assets, and their talents? There's no mandate to include any of that in our HSI work. There's no mandate to be intentional about it. So I think about how the state mandated us to do the student equity work, and it mandated us to call it out, and it mandated us to design something to address it. Why don't we have that same mandate from the Department of Education for HSI? It's good to get the money. It's better to require that we are intentional about how we're using the money for the cocurricular components and other initiatives, which I think is where we're falling short.

And I'm not saying take away the money. I'm saying let's be intentional. But people aren't seeing it the way I see it.

"It's weird because Latinos and Hispanics did come out as one of the disproportionately impacted populations when we started our student equity work. But it wasn't the *most* disproportionately impacted because, in order for you to have a disproportionate impact, you need to have a gap in the surrounding population to the enrollment, to the completion, to the transfer data. So, in terms of access, we don't have a gap—Latinos and Hispanics don't have a gap in our formula. So we're enrolling a bunch of Latinos, but at the same time, our success numbers aren't great. We have geographic enrollment by default, but we aren't serving the students intentionally and calling out the need and the relevance and the importance of them being at the institution, and showing how that helps them to uplift themselves and their community. So a lot of students feel unseen, and I think it's not unique to the Latine experience. I've heard the same from our LGBTQIA+ students, our undocumented students, our veteran students—they feel very much unseen and at the margins. They don't feel a sense of belonging at the institution despite having so many Latines there. There isn't a lot of outward commitment or robust programming to highlight their uniqueness or to make them feel valued, or like we're saying, 'You matter, and you have a role here to play, and we see you.'" I look at my friends' sympathetic faces. "So I guess it would help to hear some of the ways y'all are working on that sense of belonging."

Building a Movement Takes Time

Esperanza takes a deep breath before speaking. "I know it seems like we have our shit together, but we are still a work in progress. I don't want you to get discouraged. You are doing amazing work, Connie. Keep pushing and keep being an agitator. Yes, we have made progress, but I get discouraged on a weekly basis. If you get caught up in the shiny things, you lose sight of the real transformation work that needs to happen. So yes, we have HSI in our strategic plan, but sometimes strategic plans feel like bullshit to me. Is the strategic plan a dimension of servingness? Yes. Is HSI explicitly named in our strategic plan? Yes. Do we explicitly state the need to hire faculty who look like our student population? Yeah, we do. But the entire campus culture doesn't change just by naming these things in our strategic plan. Getting the Seal of Excelencia also doesn't change the campus culture for servingness. So yes, these are important things we should do as an HSI—have an HSI website, put HSI in the strategic plan, get the Seal of Excelencia—but we still have to change the culture for servingness.

"We've put a lot of energy into STEM initiatives because, well, let's be honest, we can get money for STEM initiatives. And that is important. But I think sometimes we don't put enough resources or care into things like social sciences or humanities. We put a ton of money into our STEM areas and to the research that goes on in the hard sciences, but you just don't see that same support in these other areas. And that one's hard for me. I struggle with our priorities sometimes. We have a program for students who want to be nurses, and it's essentially a pre-nursing program. It's specifically for in-state students and specifically for students from marginalized backgrounds. It's a wraparound program, and it's really high touch. Those students are successful, and I would say that program specifically feels like it is attached to servingness. And it's really neat, but we can only accept 20 students a year. And there's only one coordinator. So sure, it is helping students, but it's such a small number that I'm like, 'Why not expand a program like that?' At the end of the year, the program just feels like a check mark the school needs when they're writing their annual report—something to show they do diversity work. But does it really change the culture? And can we actually change the culture of medicine, or nursing, or chemistry, or areas that have historically been closed off to Latine students and other students of color?" Esperanza shakes her head. "I'm not sure we can, even with all the HSI money we get for the STEM areas.

"So, yeah, we look good on paper, but these are the things I struggle with as a leader on campus who's trying to create an entire campus culture for servingness. Will it always be siloed? Will it always be the responsibility of our cultural center to do the work? Don't get me wrong—they do it well! They're dynamic, and they're doing things that are advancing servingness in ways they weren't just a few years ago. Our campus recently put money forward for our cultural center to hire licensed counselors with the cultural background of our students. We got funding to hire four counselors, one for each of our major racial-ethnic groups. And we hired a bilingual Latine counselor for our Latine students. All four counselors are housed in our counseling center, and they have a reporting line to the director of the center. They're doing some great wellness programming. But I think the biggest obstacles with mental health are the stigma and the financial barrier. But I think we've found ways to address those barriers for students. Now, that initiative was not funded by Title V or HSI grants, but it does address servingness. So yes—" Esperanza nods "—using funds from across campus to address servingness counts as doing HSI work."

"Yes—" I nod too "—but you're doing stuff focused on Latine students and their cultural wealth. Like you hired a bilingual Latine-identified counselor. My campus isn't that intentional. We would be fine with hiring a Black counselor, which we should do, but that's all we'd get to do. We could check the equity box if we did that. So that's the difference between your campus and mine. We don't have HSI in our strategic plan. We don't have an HSI website. We don't have that level of intentionality. So I do appreciate you saying that those things alone don't make you an HSI, but I don't even have those elements to show we're becoming Latine-serving.

"But you're right, Esperanza," I say. "We do have the state backing us in this work, so that's a benefit. For our funding, we now have a formula that's based on the students we serve and whether they're meeting the benchmarks that the state says are important, which are around persistence, completion, and transfer. If we're meeting them for the disproportionately impacted populations, then we get certain dollars. If we're not meeting them, then we get penalized certain dollars. Previously our funding was based on the institution's enrollment, where if you have five students, you get funded for five students. But now we get funded a portion of our money for those five students. And another portion of our money is funded based on whether those five students are successful or not. So those benchmarks are linked, again, to what the state is asking us to do as an institution, as a community college. Don't just enroll students, make sure they're successful in whatever goal they intended—which is good. But if we're not doing any intentional work, specifically for our largest population, we're going to miss those marks."

"We haven't always focused on our Latinx population either," Daniel says in his comforting tone. "It's taken a long time to come into our HSI identity. But you can't give up. When I feel like we aren't making progress, I step back and celebrate the small wins. Tenemos muchos. And those things make a difference. One of the biggest events we recently had was the Fiesta Latina. We worked with different folks on campus, the community, different vendors. It was really awesome to see it come together because we hadn't done something like this before. It was really a resource fair but capped by an event. So it was educational and fun and cultural. And that's what we have to do sometimes. We worked with local Latino-based companies and vendors, which is good for them too. We had over 3,000 people come, primarily community members. We had a lot of students bring their families, establishing that connectedness, and creating that feeling of wanting to be here.

"We honestly do offer a lot to our Latino community," Daniel continues. "We just don't do a good job of selling it. We don't do a good job of promoting it. But the Fiesta Latina was an event where we were able to get so many people here on campus. We were on the radio, even Spanish radio, and Spanish TV too. So I'm proud of things like that. You know, the pride of that—something as simple as that is—that's our community really being here at our college. It all came through because of our grant funds. The college did help a bit, but it was primarily from the Title V grant funds that we were able to hold a community-based event that touched a lot of aspects of our community. Y por esas cosas, celebramos. We have to celebrate that we are doing good things"

"Yeah, you're right," I say. "We have to acknowledge the wins. What's one thing you're proud of accomplishing, Esperanza?"

She smiles. "We have a lot of good work worth celebrating and sharing as good HSI practices. I think one of the most substantial things we've done, which hits a lot more students than the pre-nursing program I talked about or the numerous mentoring programs we've launched, is the redesign of the general education curriculum. Our provost led those efforts, so it's had a lot of buy-in from deans and faculty. His office developed a whole new curriculum approach and trained faculty to redesign their curriculum through the lens of educational liberation and social justice. Faculty could opt in to completely redesign some of the courses that either they teach or that their colleges teach, depending on how they were structured. Faculty were required to participate in a series of summer training programs, and they were taught about a theoretical approach to curriculum redesign and provided with resources to do it. They didn't have to completely revamp what they were doing, but they could participate and work with coaches to look at their curriculum to see where they could maybe shift things to be more culturally relevant.

"So I do feel like there's been some shift, especially in the last three years. I don't know the exact stats on it, but they restructured a few hundred courses, mostly within gen ed courses, which is what a lot of our first-year and second-year students are taking. They really came at the redesign from a social justice perspective and used evidence-based practices to revamp the courses. The summer program for faculty included training on high-impact practices, offering faculty ideas for embedding them into their courses. And they even talked about liberatory learning outcomes for individual courses and gave faculty ideas for measuring those types of outcomes in their classes. That's been a huge shift to something we've never seen before. And it happened because of our HSI efforts. My office didn't initiate it, but we supported it. So I feel like that's been a big win.

"The other thing I'll say is that the HSI directors across the US have a strong network. And we learn a lot from each other. We recently met on Zoom and discussed good upper-level leadership practices, because although we have director roles, many of us still have a whole layer of administrators above us who we must manage up, which is hard. But that's almost a requirement of the job at this point—you must be able to manage your administrators if you want to see real change. We're here leading from the middle, so it's a skill we must acquire.

"Some of the things I heard from my colleagues were about what their presidents do to support HSI work. And one was that the president ensures a seat at the literal table for decision-making. So this HSI director sits on the president's cabinet, which is essentially all the VPs of the university, and she is part of that circle. This director makes decisions alongside other VPs, and the president's cabinet also participates in board meetings. So she talked about giving HSI updates at the board level and including the work that her office is building. And the board members appreciate the updates because they learn about HSI, and they can feel confident in the ROI because they know the work is being done in this area. She said she sees it as a blessing to be in the president's cabinet and to have contact with the board because as a result there's more attention on the work. And if she asks for meetings or support with initiatives to be taken on by other departments, she can say, 'This is what the institution is doing.' So that was cool to hear. But I don't sit on the president's cabinet. My office reports to the Office of Equity and Belongingness. Our VP, my boss, sits in the cabinet.

"At the Zoom meeting, a few other HSI directors chimed in and said their campuses also have presidents that have brought the HSI conversation to the board. One of our colleagues said she was in a board subcommittee meeting, and the co-chair asked the members to consider how HSI was coming into their decision-making and how they were going to keep HSI a focus throughout the year. My colleague lit up as she told the story, because that is true progress for many of us HSI directors, when we see growth across the campus, especially in the board. And she said the board is following the strategic plan, which specifically lays out what the 'S' in 'HSI' looks like for them.

"So," Esperanza says, "we really need our presidents to support our work and make sure they provide us with access to important spaces and groups, like the board of trustees. But there was also a conversation about how presidents can become HSI-minded. And that was interesting because there is not one way. Sometimes it must come from their peers or the associations they're a part of, and not from us. One of my colleagues said his president participated in a series of workshops hosted by the American Council on Education, and that was when he encountered HSI work. I guess the workshop shared a practice brief about servingness, and so the president came back to campus asking, 'What does it mean to serve? What does the "S" mean in "HSI?"' And at that point the president charged a task force with these questions. So maybe you need to send your president to ACE for training so they'll learn about HSIs."

I sigh. "It sounds good in theory, but I don't even know where my president and VPs get training from. I wish they would go to the COLEGAS conference."

"My president doesn't attend any conferences," Daniel says. "I wish he did. He just expects us to attend and bring back the information. So I think it really is our job to be advocates for HSI and servingness. I think nowadays a lot of the job of the Title V directors, or if you're lucky to have an HSI director—today those jobs include the advocacy piece. Yes, you have to manage the grant and implement the grant. But at the end of the day, you do have this unique responsibility to represent the voices of Latinx students on campus. And that's what you have to do, even as the dean of equity. It's your job."

I nod. "Y'all are right. This is why I needed to see y'all—so I could talk through these issues. I feel so alone at times because I'm not in the national HSI conversations as much as you are. But I probably should be. Thanks for this strategy session." I smile. "I love you both."

"Oh, we love you too," Esperanza says. "And I feel like we all need some alcohol now that we've had our coffee." We all laugh.

The Leaders We Need in HSIs

Two days later. I arrive to campus early, feeling reenergized for the HSI work that needs to happen on my campus. I took the conversation with Esperanza and Daniel to heart, and I'm ready to conceptualize a more intentional plan for my campus. I'm not the dean of HSI, but I am the dean of equity, and HSI is equity work. So I'm going to continue pushing for intentionality in our HSI efforts. I open a new email and address it to the colleagues on campus whom I know I can rely on to do intentional equity work. I enter the subject line "Servingness Coalition" and then write the email, inviting my coconspirators to join me on a new initiative to elevate servingness for Latine students. I do have the power to convene a small group of people on campus. I do have the power to give them a focused task to become more intentional in our HSI work. I do have the power to engage them in conversations about community cultural wealth. After talking to Esperanza and Daniel, I realized I've been trying to push for change on my own, and that is partially why I've failed. But there are people on campus who can and will support our HSI efforts if we make our efforts a priority. My supervisors don't micromanage me, and they'll allow me to pursue new areas of our equity work. I just have to convince people that Latine students face inequities on this campus, and I'll start with this small group.

5

Barriers and Resistance to Change

I am curious about our general resilience as social justice actors in a traumatizing world, and as collectives of people shaping the next phase of human evolution.
—adrienne maree brown, *Emergent Strategy: Shaping Change, Changing Worlds* (2017)

THERE IS EXTENSIVE RESEARCH about how organizations change and specifically about how colleges and universities change (Kezar, 2009, 2010; Kezar et al., 2011; Kezar et al., 2018; Kezar et al., 2025; Kezar & Eckel, 2002a, 2002b; Kezar & Lester, 2009). Within the literature on change there is also information about barriers to change. Based on 15 years of research, Kezar (2009) laid out a series of obstacles, including the presence of too many change initiatives on campus, which makes it difficult for most constituents to know about these initiatives or care about them. The sheer number of initiatives leads to additional barriers, such as a lack of synergy, despite the fact that many change ideas on campus could bolster and support each other. Moreover, the cacophony of initiatives makes it difficult to prioritize and dedicate both human and economic resources. Kezar (2009) goes on to list leadership turnover as a major barrier, arguing that deep change takes 10–15 years, while most presidents and leaders turn over in 5–7 years, with new leaders entering the campus holding their own ideas and often an unwillingness to adopt existing efforts. Other obstacles include distrust of the administration, power struggles, limited resources, and lack of incentives (Kezar, 2010; Kezar & Eckel, 2002a).

Within the HSI literature, scholars have also described difficulties in embracing an HSI identity that could be classified as barriers to change. Some have argued the exclusion of HSI and a stated desire to serve Latine students from the campus's mission and vision statements are major barriers (Andrade & Lundberg, 2018; Contreras et al., 2008; Garcia, 2023). A misalignment between the stated goals and objectives for serving Latine students in the strategic plan and the measures and practices used to embrace servingness on campus is also a barrier, as is the outright omission of HSI and servingness from the strategic plan (Flores & Leal, 2020; Garcia, 2023; Malcom-Piqueux & Bensimon, 2015). Squire and Liu (2022) documented some challenges that Northern Arizona University faced on its journey toward becoming an HSI, most notably those due to presidential turnover and competing priorities.

Although some barriers to change for HSIs are similar to those noted in organizational-change literature, many are unique to HSIs. For example, scholars have argued that a deep commitment to neoliberal logics is an obstacle toward embracing an HSI identity grounded in social justice (DeTurk & Briscoe, 2020; Doran, 2015). Moreover, white supremacy haunts many HSIs, making it difficult to advance servingness. Ortega et al. (2023) interviewed six Latine administrators at two- and four-year HSIs, and they shared that in order to succeed in their roles, they had to adopt white normative practices. This means they had to code switch from their cultural ways of knowing and language to conform to white standards. They also dealt with sabotage and racial bias from their white colleagues and intragroup animosity from other Latine colleagues on campus. Doran and Medina (2017) described outright racist concerns from some faculty members at one striving HSI about enrolling Latinx students who do not "value education." Using a case study approach, Scott et al. (2022) laid out the ways whiteness continues to be the backdrop to HSIs. Scott and colleagues found that when white administrators on campus were concerned with how becoming an HSI would affect white students, the campus moved toward a rhetoric of "all" as a tool of white appeasement. They also described how staff and faculty of color disproportionately carried out the HSI labor and how there were minimal metrics of accountability for servingness.

Barriers to change are important to acknowledge so that HSIs can address them head-on when they arise. The initiative fatigue that Kezar (2009) noted often comes up as a reason that HSI efforts are slow, yet I argue servingness can accompany other initiatives on campus. For example, adopting a servingness approach to transforming math curriculum can complement a state mandated equity plan that identifies inequities in math outcomes for Latine and Black students. These efforts are not mutually exclusive. Other barriers may be more difficult to address, like white supremacy, but acknowledging oppressive racialized systems is necessary in HSI work. Lack of accountability is also a huge barrier when it comes to HSI transformation, especially since the federal government does not hold Title V and Title III recipients accountable for advancing servingness beyond the stated goals and objectives of awarded grants. And as we know, some Title V and Title III grants are completely race evasive or Latine-ghosting—meaning, they do not pursue goals and objectives that focus on Latine students (Aguilar-Smith, 2021; Flores & Leal, 2023; Vargas & Villa-Palomino, 2018). Yet Arellano Jr. et al. (2022) provide accountability measures that can address barriers to change and lack of transparency in HSI grant work. Suggestions include creating an HSI website, sharing HSI reports with the campus community, documenting the campus's HSI history, and including students in HSI work. Regardless, these barriers remind us that resilience is essential for change, and "perhaps our most beautiful, miraculous trait" (brown, 2017, p. 126).

Documenting Barriers to Change in HSI

This chapter's counterstory is about the barriers to change that educators and leaders face as they commit to grounding their HSI efforts in servingness. Previous chapters focused on the levers of change, the processes that lead to change, and the leaders who drive change, but we must also acknowledge the barriers because they are abundant and can keep us from actualizing a Latine-serving identity. They often prevent HSIs from enacting servingness across the educational environment and hinder true transformation. This counterstory brings the realities of struggle into the conversation, acknowledging there is no progress without struggle. Emergent strategy reminds us that transformation is not linear, and facing barriers is inevitable. Leaders in the movement for change must learn from setbacks and take time to feel all the emotions that come along with this work (brown, 2017). Moreover, brown (2017) reminds us that resilience is an essential component of change—resilience in the face of barriers.

Our characters are Vanessa and Araceli, who are both doctoral students in an EdD program. Vanessa is a student services professional who works at a Hispanic-serving community college, and Araceli is an HSI project lead working at another Hispanic-serving community college. They are enrolled in a hybrid educational leadership program, where they met. Each time their cohort comes together for in-person class, Vanessa and Araceli gravitate toward one another, connected by a shared experience of frustration about their campuses' HSI efforts. As part of an assignment for their doctoral program, they conducted a pilot study about barriers to change at HSIs. Since they're both entrenched in HSI resistance on their individual campuses, they hoped this project would provide some answers and healing; they hoped to be in solidarity with their participants, to seek solutions, and to remain hopeful. They interviewed 12 participants. Now they are trying to make sense of the data, drawing on what Delgado Bernal (1998) calls "cultural intuition," including collective experiences, community memory, personal and professional experiences, and existing literature.

Research Plática con Amigas

6:35 p.m. I'm running late, so I text Araceli that I'll be a few minutes late to our 7:00 p.m. Zoom call. We're going to discuss our data and come up with a plan for the analysis and the write-up. Araceli responds with a text: "No problem, take your time." I'm relieved as I get in my car and drive the 20 minutes from campus to my house. Today was challenging, but I'm excited to talk with Araceli. I'm eager to talk about the data and to make sense of the barriers to change happening at HSIs.

7:02 p.m. I walk into my house, throw down my keys, and immediately search for something to eat in the refrigerator. I'm starving, having skipped lunch because of back-to-back meetings. I refill my water bottle and warm up the leftovers from the weekend—arroz con gandules—que sabroso! I sit down with my meal and my laptop at the kitchen table, search for the Zoom link, and enter the room where Araceli is waiting. "Hey mujer, lo siento. My day was more hectic than I hoped for."

Araceli unmutes. "No te preocupes, Vanessa. I just got on the call myself. I'm sorry your day was so hectic. Do you want to talk about it?"

I sigh. "No, I was just putting out fires all day, but I'm glad to be home and happy to talk to you about our data. And I'm starving, so I'm going to eat while we talk. I was going through the transcripts last night, and there are some really interesting stories about the struggles some folks are facing on their campuses. I want to bring these stories to light so that people know they're not alone. I often feel alone, but these interviews helped me realize I'm not. Many of our siblings at HSIs are struggling. But hey, how was your day?"

"Mine was good, pretty low-key. Nothing to complain about."

I smile and nod. "Then let's get started. Do you want to talk about the themes we're noticing in the data?" Araceli nods, so I continue. "I'm going to share a Google doc that we can takes notes on as we talk. We can also add relevant quotes to the notes." I drop a link to the document in the chat to get started.

HSI Grants Do Not Equate to Servingness

I take a few bites of arroz and feel the power of the ancestors coming back into my body. Now I'm excited for our research plática. "One thing that stood out to me," I say, "was that some participants talked about how their HSI grants do not equal servingness. In other words, just because you have an HSI grant does not mean you are an HSI. This was a common concern across participants. I also noted that some participants felt there was a lack of progress because Title V grant principal investigators, grant writers, and grant directors are not gente. And so they don't write the grant with Latinx students in mind, and instead they focus only on the Department of Education's grant priorities. Our participant Daniel shared some interesting things. He said,

> My old boss, as you can imagine by his name (Brad), is as güero as they come, but he's one of the few that recognizes that, like, 'I know my skill.' But also, he's like, once he authors it and gets the funding, then he's like, 'You got it.' Folks are critical of him often because he gets involved, but his name is known by the feds. I think it's known that people take advantage of that, as far as grant writing. Since 2000, he's been getting Title V grants every cycle they come. So, yeah, he is very much still in the vein of, like, 'Yes, get it.' Pero there has been of late just a bit of issues in our world. There are three HSI grants right now. How many gente are directors? Just me. Yeah. You have two directors on the other grant. One is more understanding and embracing than the other. It's really funny to think, how are HSI grant directors selected?

"He made a lot of good points in there, didn't he?" I say.

"Yes," Araceli says. "I have a lot of notes in his transcript. He said this pattern of white colleagues writing and directing HSI grants leads to a feeling that HSI grants should serve everyone, rather than focusing on Latinx students. Oh my gosh, I felt that. That is exactly how my campus is. We talk about equity, but we don't really do equity, especially not for Latinx students. They do the 'all lives matter' type of HSI work. It's frustrating!"

"Eso, they do that at my campus too," I exclaim. "I know at least two other people mentioned that their colleagues who write and run HSI grants are white people, and that's frustrating for them. Let me look for those two participants to see if we can build that out as a theme, something about white people leading 'all lives matter' HSI grants."

Araceli's face is flushed. She's looking pretty frustrated. "Ugh, it's so annoying," she says. "On my campus, we tried to have conversations about intersectionality with our HSI grant work that had a teacher-preparation focus. When I say 'we,' I mean the education faculty and me—the ones who were implementing the grant. When we hosted our racial equity and social justice conference, we acknowledged the different learning styles of our students, acknowledged the queer identities of our students, talked about being Black and Latinx, and how there is comradery there, and about how to support both groups of students. And when we support our Black students, we also support our Latinx students. I feel like the group that was doing the programming tried to emphasize that, but I never felt it came from our lead grant PI," she says.

"Or when we tried to push it," she continues, "it didn't go beyond our grant programming or our conference. But we wanted to have a larger impact beyond the programs. We wanted to make a difference on campus too. But a lot of these efforts, I feel like they fall on the people doing the work one-on-one with the students. I never felt like the work came from our lead investigator or our administrators. It was always faculty and staff leading the effort—the brown faculty, the faculty of color that are super involved, or the classified staff that are super involved, but they have five different jobs. I always felt like those efforts didn't leave that area. It stopped at the staff, the faculty doing the work, and same within the grant. Our white PI, who is the lead investigator on the grant, was just signing checks, and we were there to make it happen. But there comes a point where you're just tired, burnt out, and you're just like, 'I'm going to do what I can with the resources I have.' And I think that's one of the hard parts because I don't have a lot of power. I'm not an administrator."

"Period." I look up from taking notes. "I feel like our participants talked about that too—that administrators and grant PIs don't understand what HSI is or what Latine students need to succeed, and so they expect staff and faculty, and usually staff and faculty of color, to do the work. But we're not rewarded for it. It's just expected because we're Latinos ourselves."

[Author's interlude: I'm not saying white people can't write and lead HSI grants, but they need to be aware of their own racial biases and privileges, and they should center and elevate Latine people in the work. In this study, participants were most concerned with HSI grant proposals and projects that were Latine-neutral or Latine-ghosting; meaning, Latine students were not the focus.]

While Araceli nods, I quickly finish off my arroz con gandules. "Did you read Margarita's transcript?" I ask. "Even though her campus had a Latine Title V director, he didn't have a vision for HSI or servingness. Margarita said,

> We haven't had a Title V director with vision. Our new director hasn't really understood what HSI means until recently. So we're slowly seeing change. The new director recently had a title change. And I think they've been going through some self-discovery. I think they're rethinking in that way. Sometimes I don't believe I'm radical, but this is radical work we do every day. We could go from there and maybe be that push for him sometimes and say, 'Hey, have you thought of it this way? Or we should rethink that.' He thinks professional development means a speaker in front of you. I believe professional development should also be hands on. So when I provide professional development, I teach cultural things about the region. This is my Homelands, and we have rich traditions. And I get to tell that story and how other people have that parallel experience. And I get to remind participants how those traditions sometimes get cut off, especially on our campus. So I push our Title V director and help him to understand this HSI grant work is personal. And it's political.

"Uff, that part!" I say.

Araceli shakes her head. "Yes, that's how I feel. I'm constantly teaching everyone. But that gets so tiring!"

I respond with a heart emoji. We're quiet for a few minutes as we both scroll through the transcripts.

"I think there are some other HSI grant related things that came up," Araceli says. "Michelle, an HSI grant director, talked about a lack of consistency across HSI grants. She said,

> We have a new grant, but I'm not a part of it—we're very separate. We don't work together. And my biggest concern is—imagine all these Title V grants we've had. Why not work, like, collaborate with each other and say, 'This has worked for us—now, tag, you're it. Go ahead and continue our efforts.' I'm also sad because I feel like the Title V grant I'm under will end soon. Imagine all the effort we're putting in. The same folks are not always on the grants. I see value in not having the same folks because you get different ideas and different lenses. But my hope would be that the mission remains and the work we're putting in now remains. I always worry that we don't work together. We don't, we don't.

"I can see a theme building here," Araceli says as she scrolls through the transcript. "On page 21, Michelle continues and says,

> The other thing is that the vice president, who was really invested in the grant, decided to take a job in a different department. Now she works for the judicial department. And things radically changed when she left. I had to go to the Title V task force, which was reconstituted among current leadership, and say 'What is it that you all want? And how are we going to get there?'

"So there is a theme about lack of consistency across HSI grants," Araceli says, "or lack of institutionalization when people leave, or something about individual people carrying the HSI work."

I nod. "I remember Elizabeth had similar concerns. Let me find her transcript." I scroll the document for a moment. "Here it is. Elizabeth, who is not HSI staff but supports HSI efforts, said,

> Our HSI director, before she left, I would partner with her, and it was actually really cool. She would buy paletas with the little HSI budget she had, and she'd be like, 'Come celebrate HSI week and bring donations.' And whatever money was generated from that, we would add it to our DACA fund for our undocumented students. So it was awesome. But again, she left, and that's gone. We have other programs that are cool, but I'm not sure they're getting institutionalized. We have a program that offers supplemental instruction for students in gateway STEM courses—so really supporting students in that area. We have a

> lending library for students that supports them by offering the books they need. And we also have tutoring opportunities. I think that it's all grant funded—our grants are putting on these opportunities. Through one grant, we have a writing specialist and a math specialist, and they're there to provide those services. But then what happens when these grants end? What happens when these people leave? Are those services for students just going to go away? We've asked as a community what's going to happen, or what's going to be institutionalized. But those issues haven't been talked about. What's going to happen with these resources when these grants end isn't something that's been decided or shared.

"So Elizabeth was also concerned about institutionalization," I say, "and what happens when HSI grant leaders leave campus—similar to Michelle."

Araceli jumps in. "I like that theme, and I can relate to it. Our part-time education faculty on our grant left—she now works for the state. And she left because it was very frustrating that sustainability—institutionalization—was not occurring. I think it was a case of, you know, when you're passionate about something, but you're also like, look, I'll keep fighting for this, but at some point I'm going to have to move on because I also need to look after my own long-term mental health. I think that was her situation. So she left, and I don't blame her. We launched efforts to train and support our students prior to transfer, and we called the four-year institutions our students transfer to, and we tried to create a seamless pathway for them. That was the goal with this—to prepare our students, our teacher pathway students for their next step. And we've been trying to find partner schools, which is one of the goals of the grant—to find a partner school to push our students through smoothly so they don't have to apply to a million places, and make it more automatic. But I feel like it isn't our efforts that are preventing that partnership. It's at the administrative level. The colleges can't come to an agreement. So once the issue reaches the deans, that's where it stops. Because at the administrative level of presidents, VPs, a problem always arises. So we never get past VPs in the partnership. And for students, that pathway that we're trying to seamlessly create, it's not possible."

We sit in silence for a few minutes, continuing to read through the transcripts until Araceli says, "I'm having trouble finding data about this, but one thing I see on our campus is that HSI grant implementation happens in silos. And even when the grant team is working with other offices on campus, only the HSI grant team knows, and the work goes unnoticed, despite the fact that the HSI grant team is doing more for the campus than what is stated in the grant. For example, we started working with our tutoring center to increase the number of tutors available for students in diverse areas of academics, areas that typically wouldn't provide a tutor. We started providing tutors for education students, since that was the focus of our grant. But we were also funding the tutors that provided English as a second language tutoring, hoping to create support for students learning English so then they could move on as credit students, because many of them are Latinx students. And we were working with the noncredit office as well to support their efforts. But I just wish there was more recognition of the indirect work we were doing." Araceli frowns. "Oftentimes I felt like the only thing that was seen was the teacher pathways stuff, because that's directly supported by the DHSI Title V efforts."

She pauses for a moment. "But I think it would be cool to discuss how the tutoring services also tie back to the teacher pathway efforts. The Title V funds are supporting these campus tutoring efforts. And when you discuss tutoring, it feels like its own separate issue. We're using just the funding source from the federal government, and the tutoring service is never tied together with anything else. It's like, 'Oh, we're supporting the noncredit office by helping with the faculty and by helping with tutoring.' Another issue is the success coaching—how I would meet with students one on one, and how it all ties together. But right now, everything operates as siloes. So I feel like, even though this HSI funding is supposed to be moving the campus forward and institutionalizing efforts that work, everything is still its own thing, and our worlds don't collide."

I nod again. "I see Michelle also talked about that. Her quote on page 22 says,

> I don't know that Mountain State knows what's happening beyond what I'm doing with the grant. My colleagues are like, 'Oh, we have a Title V grant. We're doing HSI.' And I'm like, 'No, we're not doing HSI.' I envision doing HSI as being something vibrant. I mean, I don't envision mariachis and salsa in the pit, although that would be a good time. But I don't think people on campus understand what it means to be an HSI.

"I think what Michelle is saying is similar to what you're saying, Araceli. I suggest the theme be something like 'people think HSI is only about grant stuff.'"

People Don't Understand HSI as a Concept

Araceli agrees as she continues to scroll through the transcripts.

"Let's keep looking for data about HSI-grant-specific barriers," I say, "but also turn to the larger conversation about HSI understanding. I know you and I have talked about that in the past. My campus lacks a campuswide understanding of what it means to be an HSI. And the grant activities are like checkboxes. For example, we hosted a Latinos and AI event. OK, but it was the first year it was held, so you can't count that as an ongoing approach to meeting the longstanding criteria for serving Latinos. It's like, 'Oh, you need a STEM program? Well, it just conveniently happens that in September we had a Latinos and AI event. We had 10 students show up. Check.' But that's not sustainable. That's not looking at it at the macrolevel, which is what the HSI grant funding calls for. The grant funding provides more than enough to redesign, re-engineer, re-create, and restructure. And there's nothing happening at that level. It's the institution looking in their toolkit and saying, 'What do we already have? We need something that fits HSI. Oh, use this. OK, perfect. Check.'

I'm on a roll now. "The administration doesn't get it. I think the fundamental problem with HSI is that they embrace the popularity, the status, the high class, the association of HSI. But when it comes down to the tactics and the everyday programming and the implications of what the programming will need to be further expanded, it's a no. No, we can't do it. We don't have money. Like, really? For Latinx Heritage Month programming, they invited Latinx food vendors but didn't want to pay for the food. It was a Latinx Heritage Month celebration event for students and community members. In any other setting, I think paying for food is the norm. When we compare this type of large-scale student programming with others on campus, we see there is always some type of free food we offer students, such as a food ticket to redeem on a first-come, first-served basis. It was unfortunate that students received a conflicting message—we celebrate your heritage, but you have to pay for your own food. For other student events on campus, you don't have to pay—it's free because it's for all students. What message are we really conveying when we won't pay for Latinx-led and Latinx-focused events with HSI grant funds, but we will pay for other things?

"Recently I learned they're sending some of our instructors to a national curriculum training, which is fine. But how is that tied to HSI? Teachers need to understand how to teach Latinxs in the classroom, but the training isn't Latinx-focused. So they're using the HSI grants to justify the spending of sending these administrators and faculty to the training, but that doesn't do anything for our Latinx students. But it's like, they want to take the credit for the stuff us Latine staff are doing but won't provide Title V funding or use the grant money for Latine-focused efforts." I pause and take a breath. "Sorry, let me get off my soapbox."

Araceli laughs with me. "It's all good, girl," she says. "I'm with you. I see in the transcripts Lucia talked about a lack of understanding of HSI too. She said,

> I would say one thing we don't do yet, which I think needs to be done, is to really talk about 'Why choose an HSI? What's better about being at an HSI? Not just what is it, but why would I want to attend one?' And I think actually that needs to be on the regular admissions page if it isn't already—not just for Latinx students but for non-Latinx students. We need to explain what the advantages are of being at an HSI. Because I

> think that's also one of the constant battles. People think, 'Well, you just care about Hispanic students, you don't care about any other students.' And that's not true. It's just not true.

"She said more about that," Araceli says as she scrolls a bit. "Yeah, she also said,

> I do think that we're constantly grappling with whether we should say our focus is Latinx students, or we should stay broad. At the end of the day, our goal is to uplift all our students, not just Latinx students, right? But I keep arguing that we need to stay focused on Latinx students instead of staying so broad, because when we go broad, we don't really reach anybody, right? When we're focusing on our status as an HSI, that's a leveraging tool for focusing on Latinx. So I do believe, yes, that is constantly a conversation in terms of trying to talk about what's going on in our campus and looking at where the gaps are. And I think then, when you pair that with the DEI work and that lens as well, the focused-versus-broad issue is something we're constantly talking about. We're going to be doing some campus-wide work around that in this next academic year—as a campus, and the DEI team is pushing that. So I would say it's the conversation that happens in our HSI space a lot too.

"Well, now that I read it again," Araceli says, "it seems like Lucia is talking about how campuses are concerned that if they embrace HSI, they'll only be serving Latinx students. Which I guess gets back to campuses' lack of understanding. Ugh, it's so frustrating to know that so many of us are dealing with these same issues, and we have these same conversations on our campuses."

I drop an angry emoji in the Zoom. "It's definitely frustrating," I say. "And there are so many stories. We only talked to 12 people, yet we heard the same stories of frustration and struggle on different campuses." We both stay quiet for a few minutes as we continue to read. "Did you read Libby's transcript?" I ask. "I feel like her story encompasses so many of these themes we're looking at."

"Yes, I interviewed Libby," Araceli says, "and she was so frustrated with the HSI process on her campus. Let me pull up one of the quotes

I highlighted in her interview. It's a long quote, so I'll share it on the screen." Araceli fumbles with her tabs for a moment and then Libby's quote appears.

> The HSI committee wasn't moving. It was like the wheels were stuck in the mud, and we weren't going anywhere. I think at that point, we were researching all the HSI universities, and I think the committee attended something on servingness. It seems like the more the HSI committee leads learn, the more our timeline or whatever we're doing changes. The leads are still learning, and when they're learning, that's how we end up doing the things we do. But I was like, this is our third or fourth year of HSI. Come on, let's do something. But nothing really happened. To me, when we became an HSI—or even when we were trying to apply for HSI and then we heard that we were almost there—back then, I was like, this is our time. We should be able to do more things. And at the onset the mood was like, okay, let's meet. And so we'd meet, but then the work became about dealing with one issue after the other. The website was next. OK, we've updated the website. But now because of HSI, we need to make sure it's translated. Well, what kind of Spanish do we need? Because there's all these different kinds of Spanish, and we need to be blah, blah, blah. We would get stuck on certain things. And I'm like, 'OK, make the website, and we can work on the translation as we go, and we can just keep moving.' But a lot of people tend to get stuck on these smaller things, and they can't let go of them. Especially the language, which is important, but at the same time—let's keep moving. Because I think we could do more. I think even if we do have hiccups, we should keep the momentum going.

"That was the quote I labeled as 'wheels stuck in the mud,'" Araceli says. "I can relate to that. My campus has had our wheels stuck too." She continues to scroll through Libby's transcript and then stops again. "Here's more on that theme.

> We don't talk as a committee, which I think is exactly the problem—we don't talk about those kinds of things as a general committee. In those meetings, the updates are just, like, 'How are you doing? OK.

> This is the HSI update, and this is what we've been doing.' And that's it. Then we come together as the smaller committees, and we get assigned tasks. But then there's often some kind of obstacle, like last time we left off as we were going over our findings. Summer hit in the middle of that, and so we still haven't come together to meet. So it's just been nonideal.
>
> And then the DEI folks—I mean, I love them to death because they're the ones who appreciate the work I do—but they're off doing all these different things, going to the HSI conference, traveling to all these places to learn about HSI. So they're never here. I don't like to be blunt, but I get tired of waiting and being understanding. I understand you've got to do this, and I understand that so-and-so needs this, and I understand, I understand. I'm tired of understanding. It's very slow. Slow, trudging along. But I just keep going. What's the expression? A little bit of progress is still progress, right? Even though I don't like how slow it's going, it's still progress. I just have to think about it that way sometimes.

"She seems to have some hope toward the end," Araceli says. "She's trying to remind herself that small progress is progress. But then she goes on to say

> I like that they're even looking at servingness as a component. I'm glad, but I'm hesitant—I don't know if that's the right word. I feel like, yes, we're doing stuff, but it's Hispanic Heritage Month. After this, what's going to happen? Are they going to drop the ball again? Are we going to continue to talk? We still haven't really met as an HSI committee. I think we met once, but it was just to lay out the status quo—like, this is what we're doing. But I think, no, we need to meet, and we need to put actual things down, actionable items about how we're going to serve these students. We need to think of more than just how we want the Seal of Excelencia, so what are we going to do? No. What are we doing to serve the students, and what are some actionable items we can work on so we can reach these students?

"Never mind," Araceli says. "She only has a little bit of hope and then loses it again." We both laugh. Araceli scrolls again. "Oh," she says, "this Libby quote touches on what we were talking about with Lucia's data, about the fear of only focusing on Latinx students, and what the message is to other racial groups. Libby says,

> This is just hearsay, and I'm not sure what happened, but from what I heard, some Black students were saying, 'What about us?' And I was thinking, I thought we were trying to serve the Hispanic population. So a lot of the talk became about how we can make our campus inclusive. Let's not call it HSI for Hispanics because people will think that's all we are. But I was like, 'It's called that for a reason.' And so it became too inclusive. That's what I think. The way I understood it was that then they wanted people to ask for money, to look for funding, because now we're HSI, so go for the funding. Because that's a big thing—funding grants—and you get kudos for all the grants you can get.

"Let me make some notes about those thoughts," Araceli says, then she stops sharing her screen.

"That's an important quote," I say. "I think others talked about the same thing—this idea that campuses are reluctant to focus only on Latinx students because other racial-ethnic groups might feel left out. Let me see if I can find a good quote." A few minutes of silence pass as we scroll through the transcripts. "There are so many quotes that seem connected to all the other quotes we've been discussing. This is so hard. How are we going to narrow things down?"

"I know, right?" Araceli says. "But this is all important stuff, and I want to be able to convey it. This is also really healing to know we're not alone. Maybe we should start a support group for frustrated HSI employees." We both laugh, but it's not a bad idea.

We Lack the Infrastructure for Servingness

It's getting late, but I'm feeling motivated by this project. "Can we discuss quotes and themes about the general infrastructure for servingness?" I say. "I noted that issue as a theme—how campuses don't have the capacity to advance servingness with their current infrastructure." Araceli agrees, and we both scroll and read.

"I've highlighted a few quotes about HSIs shutting down programs that have historically done servingness," Araceli says, "like cultural centers and ethnic studies. Here's a good quote from Margarita. She said,

> We collapsed the multicultural center and combined it with the international office. Now, as you know, the multicultural office serves a whole different way than an international office does. And those two sets of students maybe don't have the same needs, right? But they believed that, since those are people of color and international students are people of color too, then it would all just work out. And they didn't even talk about the historically underrepresented folks from this area or from across the United States that they just diminished, like the undocumented students. They didn't understand how that experience doesn't compare to the privilege of being an international student, and they just put all those people into one room.

"That point seems significant," Araceli says.

I nod. "Yes, I'm pulling up a few more quotes like that. Natasha stated,

> I remember—was it 10 years ago? They were trying to close down the Mexican American studies program. And the students protested. Luckily for the university, they heard the students, and they didn't close it, but it's not a priority program. It's been around for over 40 years, and so many Latinx students take those classes.

"And then here is one more I'm adding to the Google doc," I say. "This one is from Gudelia.

> I don't know the backstory to why the Center for Latino Studies split, but because they split, the arm of the president's office is really the Center for Critical Studies. So that really puts the Center for Latino Studies further away from influence, and it's just siloed. Now most of the HSI efforts are happening under the Center for Critical Studies. And that's fine, but the director is Black, and the president is Black, so they don't prioritize HSI and Latine students as much.

> The previous director of the Center for Latino Studies tried. She tried, and she actually brought all the Latino faculty members together. She invited us to dinner with other professors from the center and kind of said, 'Hey, this is an HSI, but y'all are going to need us, and we all need each other, and so how can we work together and support one another?' So she held a writing group over the summer. And because we don't have a lot of tenure-track Latino faculty members, she opened it up to folks who identified as Black as well. I was in that writing retreat. It felt like she understood solidarity, and she was working toward that. I don't know what happened in the past, but I think the president identifies more with the Center for Critical Studies, and he just relies on them. Maybe it was different before, but it seems like the Center for Critical Studies is closer to the president and is more important in that sphere of influence. So the Center for Latino Studies is just disempowered.

"I interviewed Gudelia," I say, "and she was really frustrated. She didn't really know what was going on with the two centers, but from her perspective, disempowering a historically Latino space was not good for an HSI."

Araceli clenches her fists in frustration. "Yes, that happened here too. Our Latino center was collapsed into another center. It was so infuriating. How can we be an HSI without those spaces?"

"I know, yo sé," I say. "It's so backward to shut down and disempower spaces that have historically been serving Latine students. I also noted that Lucia talked about a similar but slightly different problem, which is that her campus doesn't have cultural centers or ethnic studies. And as a small campus, they don't have the resources to develop Latine-specific spaces. She said,

> We don't have all those things like ethnic studies, cultural centers, and TRIO.[1] The thing is I don't know if we're ever going to get them. So in order to move into that other box where we're Latine-enhancing, we're

1. For information about TRIO programs, see US Department of Education. (2026, February 4). *Federal TRIO programs*. Office of Postsecondary Education. https://www.ed.gov/about/ed-offices/ope/trio

> going to have to think beyond those typical structures. Because a lot of those typical structures are going to come from being in a larger institution that has more financial resources and just has more students in general. I know those are mostly state schools and bigger places who have been around. I mean, we've been around a long time, but those are public institutions more so than private institutions.

"This is an interesting perspective," I say. "The servingness research stresses that HSIs should have ethnic studies and cultural centers, but what if the campus doesn't have the capacity? Lucia also talked about having a small student enrollment, so there may not be enough students to fill ethnic studies classes."

"Yes, that is a huge barrier," Araceli says. "We've struggled to launch our ethnic studies program after the state mandated it because we don't have enough faculty with that type of expertise. But I think Dr. Garcia's book suggests that all curricula should be culturally relevant and responsive to Latine students. So it's not always about having specific ethnic studies programs but rather using those concepts for other classes. And that's what we tried to do with our education classes—add those core ethnic studies concepts to the classes. But we had a Title V grant to do it. So Lucia's point is valid—it takes money and resources."

"It's always about money," I say. "I see Lucia also talked about the lack of funding to institutionalize grant efforts. Here on page 32, she said,

> If there's something we were trying out in the STEM areas, and we want to replicate that in other fields of study across the college, then there needs to be other opportunities for funding to do that. I mean, as you know, we're a small private college, and we don't have a lot of students. We're broke sometimes. So finding those resources to replicate the good work we're getting as a result of that funding is hard.

I notice myself nodding. "This is connected to the difficulty of institutionalizing efforts—that issue we already have some notes on. At this point, I feel like all these themes are interconnected. Which makes sense. But going through these quotes and identifying specific themes is hard because they overlap."

"Well, I guess we're gonna write a really good paper then," Araceli says, and we both laugh. "Let's discuss a few more quotes, and then I have to jump off the call to help my mom with some paperwork. Gotta translate for her."

"Mira, these eldest-daughter duties never end!" I say. "Pero yes, let's find a few more and then log off for the evening. I'm going to drop a few more quotes about the lack of culturally relevant curriculum as a barrier to advancing servingness into our document, but we don't have to discuss them all right now. This one from Rosalía is interesting though.

> I think my department is at a very weak point where they're trying to juggle everything and trying to rewrite a curriculum. But I don't think that they have specific objectives or that they have identified what it is they're supposed to be writing in the curriculum. They've started several classes about BIPOC performers in theater, which they're trying hard to put together but, as my faculty colleague told me, 'You and I can't do all the change in the department, other people have to try as well.' They can't just say, 'Oh, I'm reworking the curriculum,' or 'We're trying to rework the classes that are offered in the next season or the next semester for the students to be more diverse,' but then they can't identify what being diverse is.
>
> Do they actually know before they try to rewrite the curriculum or to rewrite what classes are being offered? Can they identify what diverse is? Is that even being identified first, or are they just working because they got hit by this letter that told them they had to be more inclusive? Is that the reason they're doing this work? So I'm really confused by what's going on.
>
> The other thing is that they're secretive about this whole curriculum rewriting. They only vaguely talk about it in our faculty meetings. They're the same way with their research too. Everyone's required to do research as faculty, but nobody shares what the research is, and that's

just the way everything is. Instead of them coming out and saying, 'Well, we're not quite sure how we need to be more inclusive with our curriculum,' they stumble around and try to write something, and it goes in no real direction.

It seems like the curriculum rewriting has been going on for over a year, and it's nonstop. There's no finish to it, no end. So do they even know what they're doing, or do they just say they're rewriting it to try to make everybody happy? It's really strange.

"So much to unpack," I say. "I don't even know where to begin! I think we can come back to her whole interview the next time we meet because she shared a lot of frustration and confusion throughout her interview. She talked about being a woman of color in a predominantly white department and feeling left out of diversity and inclusion conversations." Araceli nods, and I add, "Skyler also talked about curriculum and representation of faculty in different departments. He said,

The big thing we always talk about is how we don't want to involve only those represented in Chicano studies or education, where you have your concentration of Latinx faculty. I mean, I would venture to say 50% of our faculty are in those two disciplines. Add sociology, and you might have like 75%. But yeah, it does get relegated sometimes to your ethnic studies or your Chicano studies faculty to do this work. But I'm like, 'Well, how does this go into math or calculus 1 or calculus 2, or your mechanical engineering?' They always think about curriculum redesign as content based, but is it just content based when you're thinking about engineering and the way you build things and how that might relate to people and community and society, and who can benefit from better design and more cost-effective machines?

"So I think we have to talk about curriculum and faculty in our paper," I say, "because both topics came up a lot in different ways. Back to Natasha—she talked about the lack of incentives for faculty to get involved in HSI efforts on campus, which is also important. Here's what she said.

> I think there was a call for everybody to join the HSI task force, but we have this funky rubric, and I get more credit for doing stuff at a national level. So there's no incentive for me—as much as this is important—to get involved in it. I'm tenure track, and I'm like, 'I need to get tenure, and I don't get credit for the task force.' The libraries are working on adding this to our evaluation, but it's currently not in our evaluation. As selfish as it sounds, it's possible I chose not to join the task force, but I don't remember being asked or there being a call for it.

"That is another important point," Araceli says. "Staff representation came up too. I wanted to bring up Skyler's quote because he talks about having Latine infrastructure and spaces but not having the human resources needed to run those spaces. Let me read the quote.

> The Latinx Resource Center, or the LRC, is a structure. And it has support staff. Actually it has a faculty liaison. But the director left. And there's a lack of institutional support. So you might have the structure, but the individual doesn't have the support to be successful. I think in that regard, we lost a little bit in the sense that we have the structures in place, but the support for the personnel to oversee the structures and use the structures for a benefit aren't there. So it's like we have this important crane that's helping to build this bridge, but the crane operator wasn't being supported, so they quit. And now we have a crane and supplies for a bridge, but it's not getting built.
>
> Sometimes I work in the LRC space, without a director right now. Here's an anecdote I overheard there. They paid for cool artists to do murals, but then an artist showed up and waited for two hours for someone to open up the space. No one ever came, so the artist left. This was just something I overheard because I was being chismoso listening, but it's a perfect example of what it's like there without a director to oversee everything. We have this space, and it can make a difference, but right now it's at a standstill because there's no one leading it. But that structure, assuming it gets built back up again, is very helpful. It unifies all the Latinx student orgs on campus. And the LRC also has an advisory group that works with faculty. So the HSI team is the hub for a

lot of the institutional efforts. And the Latinx Resource Center is the hub for student-related efforts. We just hired someone—I was at the interviews for them. But like I said, it was a big blow that over the summer, early fall that structure has been vacant.

"Super powerful, right?" Araceli says. "He went on to say

You might ask too much of staff, or not offer enough support, or you empower them, and then they go off and do stuff, but then it's not reciprocated. So they're like, 'You told me I could start this effort, and now I'm not getting the resources for it. So why build someone up just to break them down?' And I think institutionally there's some of that. There's a lot of shuffling of personnel. That makes it tough to make real progress. I'm trying to put my pin on it, but I don't have a good sense of why this is happening. I think reorganization always throws these types of things off. Both the reorganization of who HSI falls under, who the Latinx Resource Center falls under. Then also its priority within the division of Student Affairs and Diversity, Equity, and Inclusion. And then interim people that know they're not going to get the role permanently, so how much effort do they put into their interim work? There are various other things. But the bottom line is that when the power to make change is taken from people, they leave.

"This quote is another example of people leaving the institution and taking their servingness skills with them," Araceli says. "It's a theme! And going back to Lucia's interview, she also talked about staff turnover and how it slows down the work.

As you know, there's tons of turnover right now, all the time everywhere. So I have new people coming in and out, inviting new folks to join us in HSI efforts, and people leaving who carried different pieces of the HSI work. So then it stalls out in some areas. My hope is that having an HSI plan will help us to better articulate to our campus community what our goals are, what we're trying to do, and to engage people in the work in a clearer way so they can more easily look at what we've set out to do and say, 'OK, I think I could actually contribute in this area. This is something I want to do.'

"And one more quote from Maya," Araceli says. "She also talked about how staff resources are limited. She said,

> I'm not sure if you could sense this, but I feel like—our HSI group feels like—we want to do more, but our resources are limited. Our time is limited. Everybody that's serving in this group does it on top of their regular job. We're not getting time off or anything else for that. If we had resources to send some of us to conferences or to send students to development programs . . . I'd say that's the frustration we have. There's a lot we want to do, but we feel inhibited.

"So," Araceli says, "we have a lot more to unpack the next time we meet."

"Mira, I'm done," I say. "My brain hurts." We both laugh.

"Yeah, we just downloaded a bunch of deep stuff on our souls," Araceli says, "and now we gotta log off and wait until next time to talk about it."

I grin. "I know, I know!"

"It's all good, girl," Araceli says, smiling back at me. "Let's stop there and schedule our next meeting. I'm exhausted and hungry!"

After a wave to Araceli, I log off Zoom. But I keep scrolling through the quotes on my own. I feel connected to every person we interviewed, and honestly, I'm overwhelmed by the weight of this HSI labor. It does feel good to know I'm not alone, but no one should feel defeated by a designation that's intended to bring about positive change for Latine students on campus. I return to a quote from Margarita, who talked about how slow the process is and how her institution is just not ready.

> So that's a hard one to swallow, when the president says this is the people of the state's university, because I was made in my community, I'm built in my community, I work in my community, and this university is in my community. It's a hard thing to swallow as a Chicana that believes she's in the middle of Aztlan, right? We're in the borderlands, and what does this all mean when we're at an HSI? We're one of the oldest HSIs in the state. It's Arena State, and it's us, and where are we

Table 5.1
Barriers to HSI Transformation

Barriers Preventing HSIs from Changing	Overall Concern
HSI grants are not used to advance servingness.	Missed opportunity to use HSI grant funds to test innovative ideas for serving Latine students.
HSI grant directors are not Latine identified.	HSI grant directors do not understand or care about the specific equity and cultural needs of Latine students.
HSI grants do not focus on Latine students; they seek to serve all students.	This is a missed opportunity for equity-focused solutions to supporting Latine students.
Most educators and leaders on campus do not understand the servingness concept or what HSI means beyond 25% enrollment.	Educators and leaders on campus who do understand HSI as a concept feel isolated and alone in HSI efforts.
Educators of color are expected to do all the HSI work.	HSI work feels overwhelming and defeating; there is a lack of solidarity for HSI.
Lack of vision exists for HSI or servingness.	It is difficult to advance transformative change without vision.
Lack of consistency exists across HSI grants.	Change efforts feel disjointed.
HSI grant leaders leave campus; staff turnover slows down HSI progress; staff members take servingness skills with them when they leave.	HSI efforts are stalled or thwarted.
Lack of institutionalization and lack of funding to institutionalize grant efforts persist.	Five years of HSI work and servingness efforts are lost once grant cycle ends.
HSI grant implementation happens in silos.	This is a missed opportunity for advanced collaboration in transformation efforts.
Misconception exists that to be an HSI involves only HSI grant implementation.	HSI grants are only one dimension of servingness; some HSIs are unsuccessful at getting HSI grants, but that does not preclude them from being an HSI.
Campuses shut down programs that have historically done servingness (i.e., cultural centers, ethnic studies).	There is a need to recognize, acknowledge, and support the historical servingness work on campus.
Concern exists that if we are an HSI, we only serve Latine students.	Misconception continues about racial equity and social justice components of HSI identity.
"Wheels stuck in the mud."	There is no action attached to HSI efforts.
Campuses do not have cultural centers or ethnic studies programs.	There is no campus commitment to historical spaces of servingness and no funding to launch cultural centers and ethnic studies programs.
There is a lack of human resources; staff resources are limited.	True transformation requires human resources.
No incentives exist for faculty to do HSI work.	Asking faculty to do more than they are compensated for is unethical.
Process is slow, and the institution is not ready.	Educators and leaders get frustrated when they don't see change.

located? That's two rural institutions. What does it mean that we're the first two HSIs, but we're still underdeveloped compared to some big city universities going 500 miles an hour right now as new HSIs. And here we are, just going steady at about 50 miles an hour. But we all know the value of our institution. We know we could be like those bigger universities. But sometimes we have to go back into ourselves and realize that it's not our time right now, and we've got to wait for the next leadership. And that's hard.

I stop reading and close my laptop. I sit back in my chair and look up at the ceiling, thinking. I'm not sure what to do with all these quotes, but I know how important it is to share these stories. I sit up, open my laptop again, and start a new Google document to summarize the barriers to change we've identified so far (table 5.1).

6

Envisioning the HSI-Thriving Era

One core practice of resilience is transformative justice, transforming the conditions that make injustice possible.
—adrienne maree brown, *Emergent Strategy: Shaping Change, Changing Worlds* (2017)

I HAVE USED A STORYTELLING METHOD to lift the voices of the HSI struggle. First, I argued that HSIs are in transition, and then I brought the stories of transition to life. The voices that emerged are from the grassroots; they are the voices of the people who are committed to change. The characters represent the HSI changemakers in the transitional era, those who know that enrollment, eligibility, and grant seeking and grant getting are insufficient markers of servingness. Each character helped us understand what it looks like to be a part of the HSI movement during the transitional era, with a focus on grants as levers of change, the processes of change (or processes of servingness), the grassroots leaders who are organizing the movement, and the barriers to change.

The stories of change are grounded in emergent strategies, and I encourage you to share these stories and learn from them. Although the stories are fictionalized, they are grounded in real-life examples of how HSIs are transitioning. The stories come from the kindred spirits in the HSI movement who are driving change in the face of enormous political, social, and economic challenges. They are leading second-order change efforts and challenging the longstanding, enduring missions of historically white-enrolling colleges and universities. Many of the efforts described in each chapter are structural; meaning, HSI leaders are trying to shift the culture of their institutions, yet they know that attitudinal and mindset shifts are essential too. Becoming HSI-minded is necessary.

In chapter 2, we saw how HSI directors have used Title V and Title III grants—some of the most important policy levers of change—to implement new campus infrastructures, develop new processes, and address the campus culture and longstanding institutional logics. These HSI leaders have actively worked to create environments where Latine students can thrive, acknowledging that persistence, graduation, and job placement are insufficient measures of a Latine-serving identity. Chapter 2 highlighted the small yet substantial changes being employed, including curriculum redesign, HSI student advisory groups, HSI logos and T-shirts, engagement with Latine community centers and families, conversations about microaggressions, and solidarity building across racial-ethnic groups. Focusing on the fractals, or small changes, has the potential to create longstanding organizational change.

In chapter 3, we learned about the processes of servingness, which are the actions, activities, and practices that HSI leaders are implementing to drive change. Of importance, the processes of servingness are intentional, with campuses deliberately adapting to the needs and identities of students rather than expecting students to assimilate into the campus. Intentional adaptation is how movement-based change works, with HSI leaders guiding organizational change by drawing on essential processes. Some of these processes include changing recruitment and enrollment policies, hiring bicultural and bilingual staff, developing a SWOT analysis, creating an HSI strategic plan, centering HSI in mission and vision statements, accessing existing human resources, creating a campus HSI narrative, developing HSI websites, and initiating cluster hiring to diversify faculty. The characters in chapter 3 expanded on many of the processes and activities discussed in chapter 2 with an essential caveat: They are doing HSI work without Title V and Title III grants.

In chapter 4, we learned from our midlevel leaders, who are often closely connected to both students and colleagues and are probably the most committed to change. They often lead with passion and corazón, figuring out how the organization works so they can change it. Our narrator, Connie, highlighted the external influences on servingness, including state-level mandates and policies that can advance equity efforts, yet she also elevated the tensions that can arise. Most importantly, she presented a real struggle in HSI work that occurs when a campus enrolls a critical mass of Latine students and falsely believes it is adequately serving them. Although providing access to higher education for the Latine community is important, that does not translate to servingness. Connie has been stifled, as many grassroots leaders are, but her colleagues convince her to work interdependently and to lean into the decentralization of college campuses. As noted in emergent strategy, change can be facilitated by authentic connections and relationships, which Connie clearly has. She notes the tactics she has used to share resources and build critical connections across programs, which form the best approach for impacting larger systems.

In chapter 5, our characters described the real barriers and challenges that HSI practitioners face on campus as they actively try to change the institution from the inside. This chapter makes it clear that organizers must remain resilient in the face of adversity. Much of the adversity stems from the lack of readiness for HSI work, lack of resources to advance servingness, lack of understanding of HSI, and lack of commitment to doing something different. Vanessa and Araceli described the frustration that arises as HSI grassroots leaders hit walls while trying to convince their campus colleagues that HSI work is everyone's job, that resources are needed, and that centering Latine students in HSI efforts does not have to be exclusionary. Yet leaning into emergent strategies reminds us that the process of change is nonlinear and iterative. As long as campus HSI organizers can remain resilient, they will observe the cycles of success and failure that are inevitable in the process. Learning from our mistakes and challenges is a necessary part of change work, while we remain committed to coalition building and collective consciousness about the goal of HSI efforts. Most importantly, chapter 5 is a call to normalize struggle in the process of change.

The transitional era is full of stories of wins and progress, and stories of challenge and struggle. Yet each story is full of hope when we look at change through an emergent strategy lens, with brown (2017) stressing that change starts with the small and builds from the fractals; it is nonlinear and iterative; it is decentralized, with each leader working interdependently to strategize and drive movement. And she reminds us to stay resilient. The HSI grassroots leaders in each story know small changes will lead to larger organizational transformation. They are intentionally planning for the adaptation that is inevitable and using collective action to drive change. And they are doing it in community, with colleagues and students on campus and with colleagues and organizations beyond the institution. They are sharing resources with their networks and building critical connections, which is how we impact larger systems. They are also remaining diligent in the face of setbacks and barriers. Each chapter was intended to normalize change as iterative and nonlinear and to show how organizing at the campus level can expand relationships in order to leverage the power needed to enact change. Collective power is the strength needed to experience a true form of liberation (Hayes & Kaba, 2023).

The next HSI era will be the thriving era—an era when HSIs will be unwavering in their commitment to enrolling, serving, educating, and empowering Latine students. In this era, students, faculty, and staff will thrive in spaces where equity and justice are valued, and institutions will thrive, receiving adequate funding and state and federal support to educate, uplift, and empower minoritized communities. I don't expect us to get there for another 25–30 years even if we work really hard and commit to becoming unapologetic HSIs. And it could take longer, as there are many barriers to change noted throughout this book. The empirical data, coupled with my lived experience as a public intellectual and consultant working directly with HSIs, provided the basis for understanding how HSIs can change—and are changing. But the vision for a thriving era is not yet actualized.

To make that vision reality, we must keep envisioning what a thriving era would look like; we must first imagine them, and we all play a part in building those futures we want to see (Hayes & Kaba, 2023). This chapter is about envisioning and *creating more possibilities* for HSI futures. And creating more possibilities is about transformative justice, which requires the disruption of the root causes of injustices (brown, 2017). In her work, brown asks us "to consider how to transform toxic energy, hurt, legitimate pain, and conflict into solutions" (p. 133). Emergent strategies combined with liberation theory provide us with a path toward thriving; one where we accept that change is a process of disrupting harm and building new liberatory futures so students can enhance their understanding of self and identity as well as expand their critical consciousness around the most pressing issues in contemporary times (Freire, 2014; hooks, 1994).

For HSIs to become spaces of justice and liberation, we require a complete transformation of colleges and universities as we know them. The counterstories throughout these chapters described the tactics used to leverage Title V and III grants to enact transformative justice, the servingness processes that can be used to transform energy and pain into progress and growth, and the struggle for transformation that leaders face. And while we often demand change by calling on the institution or the state or the federal government to enact policies that will allow us to thrive, brown (2017) reminds us the fight for justice starts with us as individuals, as families, and as communities. The characters in this book believe this deep in their hearts and souls, which is why they continue to fight despite the setbacks and challenges. The possibilities are endless if we can first envision and then collaborate to enact the world we want to see (brown, 2017). Envisioning will not be reductive, as there are many possibilities for HSIs that can be tailored and tweaked to meet the demands of the diverse students in our institutions and the needs of the regions where our campuses reside. Here I offer one vision, among many.

HSIs as Spaces of Possibility

HSIs will become a common institutional type where HSI-ness is no longer questioned. All people who interact with the campus will know it is an HSI; all students, all faculty, all staff, all administrators, all trustees, all donors, all people—they will know and actively choose to be there. Presidents, chancellors, provosts, and deans will be proud to lead an HSI and ensure employees have what they need to enact servingness: adequate pay and benefits, adequate training and professional development, and adequate time to dream and build an institution where students, faculty, and staff can thrive. People also need time to rest and recover, and that will be honored. Administrators will honor HSI efforts while empowering middle managers and change leaders to advance grassroots HSI efforts. Leadership will be collaborative and affirming and will embrace movement-based tactics such as relationship building and mutually beneficial partnerships.

We will listen to students. Not superficially but authentically, asking for their feedback on curriculum and course design, faculty representation, student services, community engagement, the campus environment, and everything they directly interact with—not through surveys that we never address but through community circles and authentic pláticas. Students will know they are valued and will bring their whole selves to the campus. They will offer their community cultural wealth, their knowledge, their language, their gifts, and their talents to a campus that is responsive to them. Students will be proud of who they are when they arrive and will be willing to grow and develop, seeking to understand themselves first before understanding others.

The mission and vision statements for the institution will unapologetically name the campus as an HSI and the Latine population as the target group, yet not the only group and not a monolithic group. We will acknowledge that Latines are white, Black, Indigenous, and mixed race; that they are sometimes US-born but sometimes not; that some are immigrants, some are undocumented, and some are from mixed-status families. We will acknowledge that their ancestors are from the Americas and the Caribbean and speak many different languages. I offer a fictional mission statement to help us imagine this possibility.

> Feliz University is a racially and culturally diverse Hispanic Serving Institution (HSI) that provides an exceptional academic experience for undergraduate, graduate, and professional students. We provide opportunities for growth and success for all students with a particular emphasis on Hispanic and Latine students who represent a diverse mix of races, cultures, and languages. We also provide access to a high-quality and affordable education for students with origins across the Americas and the Caribbean. As an HSI, we commit to educating students who want to advance democracy and justice in their careers and future endeavors. We also commit to working with local communities and businesses and to training bilingual and bicultural leaders for the region. We assume our responsibility in teaching the history and culture of Latines. We commit to the social and economic mobility of students and the community uplift of their families.

The strategic plan will name equity and justice as core outcomes for students, faculty, and staff, and it will map out a vision for moving the campus toward servingness. I offer a fictional vision for our imagination.

> Feliz University is accountable to our constituents for being innovative and inclusive in our academic efforts. We remain committed to educating our local community and the people of the state so that we can thrive. Our four strategic priorities are as follows:
>
> 1. Student success: We will ensure that all students succeed in the classroom and beyond. This will require a regular review of disaggregated outcomes, including classroom-level outcomes, departmental-level outcomes, and institutional-level outcomes by race/ethnicity, gender, and income. We will address inequities by holding faculty and administrators accountable for outcomes.
> 2. Environment of care: We will ensure that all constituents, including students, faculty, and staff, feel welcomed, accepted,

and valued on campus. This includes the curricular and cocurricular spaces on campus, where we will offer culturally and linguistically relevant experiences and opportunities to learn about and engage with racially and ethnically diverse people. We will not tolerate hate, racism, harassment, or discrimination in any form and will hold faculty, staff, and administrators accountable for these experiences.

3. Collaboration and connection: We will build relationships with constituents most committed to our mission to serve a diverse community and advance justice for minoritized people. This includes collaborations with public and private entities that can ensure the resources to fulfill our purpose and ensure equitable outcomes and experiences for all.
4. Bilingual and bicultural world: We commit to training a workforce that is bilingual and bicultural, a workforce that can serve the diversity of people in our region, state, and country. We are committed to training future health professionals, first responders, lawyers, politicians, entrepreneurs, caregivers, teachers, scientists, engineers, and public servants to serve our country through a lens of equity and justice.

The HSI identity will be apparent throughout the campus. Websites will show the vibrancy of the Latine population and include pictures of students across ethnic identities, races, languages, and cultures. Students will wear bilingual shirts that suggest pride in the institution (e.g., Somos Panthers). The campus environment and culture will feel like an HSI. There will be artwork and paintings and murals that show the vibrant Latine community thriving in history and present day. Food will help students feel at home, whether it is arroz con gandules, mofongo, arepas, yaroa, sancocho, or pozole in the cafeteria or tamales at special events during the holiday season. There will be music on campus that helps students feel as though they belong, including corridos, jíbaro, bambuco, salsa, merengue, bomba, and cumbia. There will be performances on campus that elevate the historical and cultural traditions of Afro-Latines and Indigenous Latines. And multilingualism will be the norm, including campus signage; employees and students alike will feel comfortable translanguaging.

Students will seek out the campus because of the affirming environment. They will actively apply to the campus because it is an HSI. Outreach and recruitment offices will know that mothers and abuelitas are the decision-makers in the Latine family, and these offices will ensure these family members understand the processes of admission, enrollment, and transfer. Latine families will be invited to engage with the campus for orientation, homecoming, family weekends, awards ceremonies, and graduations, all in bilingual and culturally affirming ways.

The curricula will elevate the voices, histories, and stories of Latines, Afro-Latines, Indigenous Latines, and the vibrant mix of the campus community. The curricula will be transformed—not just ethnic studies but the Math Department, the Chemistry Department, the Engineering and Computer Science Department, the Psychology Department, the Sociology Department, and the Political Science Department. Professional schools at universities and career technical programs at community colleges will train bicultural and bilingual professionals to serve the community. The School of Medicine, the School of Social Work, the School of Nursing, the School of Dentistry, the Law School, the School of Education, welding programs, automotive technology programs, construction management programs, allied health programs—all will teach courses that center the diverse, bicultural, bilingual communities students will serve, and they will ensure their graduates are prepared.

The curricula will ensure students gain knowledge of self and others while elevating their critical consciousness and healing—healing from anti-Blackness, anti-Indigeneity, anti-LGBTQIA+, anti-woman, anti-immigrant sentiments and healing from lateral oppression. The curricula will address the uncomfortable reality that oppressed people often oppress others, and it will seek to address this as a form of healing. It will help students realize the diversity within the Latine community, complicating Latinidad while allowing students to see themselves in all their complexities in the curricula. It may also address healing from previously harmful academic spaces and policies, the type that punish students for simply existing. The centering of identity in the classroom will transcend to the communities the campus seeks to serve. Future police officers and lawyers and judges will be trained in a curriculum that teaches the deep inequities in the judicial system, and the campus will intentionally train equity-minded professionals who acknowledge that systems are harmful to many populations, especially minoritized populations.

The cocurricular opportunities and student support services will similarly operate through an identity-affirming approach. They will take an intersectional approach to supporting students, understanding that students are too complex to pick one identity space, instead opting for services that recognize their complex identities and community cultural wealth. Out-of-classroom spaces will track usage and ensure students are getting what they need to succeed. The campus will grapple with equity questions around issues we know affect people of color differently, questions such as "Which groups access disability services, counseling and psychological services, food pantries, legal services, and health-care services?" and "Are there inequities in usage, and how can we address these inequities?"

There will be equity in representation across the faculty, the staff, the administration, and the board of trustees. HSIs will be Latine-led organizations. And there will be an acknowledgment of the diversity of Latines, with an elevated focus on ensuring representation of Afro-Latines, Indigenous Latines, and queer and trans Latines. Equity in representation will transcend the governance structures, including faculty and staff senates and institutional governing boards. When it comes to making decisions, the mission and vision of the campus will guide conversations, placing the livelihoods of Latines at the center, with the goal of ensuring their success and thriving within and beyond the institution. When making decisions, we will always ask, "But what does this mean for Latine students? And what does it mean for other minoritized populations?" Decision-makers will know that supporting one group does not mean excluding another. There is no limit on the pie because we can always bake more pies—or buy more conchas. Creating opportunities for one creates opportunities for others because we have an abundance mentality, not the scarcity mentality of a capitalist society. We can all thrive. There will be solidarity on campus across Black, Indigenous, Latine, and AAPI populations, and a disruption of the siloed approach to supporting diverse communities.

Local vendors and contractors will be Latine-owned and -operated. We will prioritize women- and minority-owned small businesses in the community, who can thrive off college and university business. We will create partnerships with local educational systems; create pathway programs between high schools and community colleges and four-year institutions; and create transfer-sending and transfer-receiving environments, knowing that students move through systems, many of which are also HSIs, and working intentionally to ensure a smooth transition. We will train identity-conscious educators in one HSI to serve the students in another. Pathway programs will be for undergraduate students, graduate students, and faculty and staff, affirming that we all enter the institution in transition and need support in the process. This may include training teachers to work in Hispanic-serving school districts or graduate students to become faculty in Hispanic-serving community colleges. Working collectively across systems will ensure we all thrive.

Alumni will engage with the campus, elevating the campus's long-term commitment to being an HSI and serving the diversity of the Latine population. They will wear hoodies that say Proud HSI Alum and tout that they are HSI grads. Alumni in legislative positions and other positions of power will ensure the campus's livelihood as an HSI is elevated. States will pass policies that support servingness and equity, including supportive policies for undocumented people, policies that ensure access to college-level courses, and policies that ensure the rights of women, queer, and trans people. State systems will ensure funding is available to address the needs of the largest populations on campus and the most minoritized. Federal HSI grants will be need based not competitive. A critically conscious HSI will know that neoliberalism creates class hierarchies for people and organizations, and it will work to be class-conscious.

I've laid out this vision more than once. But in reality, you must envision your own future for your HSI. What does it look like to create new possibilities on your campus for your students with your local communities in mind? What does it look like to thrive as an HSI and for all members of the campus community to thrive? To thrive is to be successful, to flourish, and to prosper in an environment that is supportive and that contributes to your growth and development. The vision of HSIs as spaces where all people are affirmed and empowered requires us to address the reality that many people are not. HSIs must also address the realities of harm while creating the futures we want to see. Affirmation, empowerment, and thriving also include healing and joy as core outcomes. The vision of HSIs as spaces of equity and justice transcends space and time and will continue into the near future. I invite you to envision this as part of your HSI movement. Visioning, dreaming, and action are core dimensions of HSIs in transition. Servingness is a feeling and an action and a process; it is transformation and healing, and it is love and cariño. ¡Que viva el movimiento!

REFERENCES

Abrica, E. J., García-Louis, C., & Gallaway, C. D. J. (2020). Antiblackness in the Hispanic-serving community college (HSCC) context: Black male collegiate experiences through the lens of settler colonial logics. *Race Ethnicity and Education, 23*(1), 55–73. https://doi.org/10.1080/13613324.2019.1631781

Aguilar-Smith, S. (2021). Seeking to serve or $erve? Hispanic-Serving Institutions' race-evasive pursuit of racialized funding. *AERA Open*, *7*(1), 1–15. https://doi.org/10.1177/23328584211057097

Aguilar-Smith, S., & Yun, J. (2023). Toward ensuring the equitable allocation of federal funding: An analysis of Hispanic-serving institutions' pursuit and receipt of Title V grants. *Education Policy Analysis, 31*. https://doi.org/10.14507/epaa.31.7281

Albert, S., & Whetten, D. A. (1985). Organizational identity. In L. L. Cummings & B. M. Staw (Eds.), *Research in organizational behavior* (Vol. 7, pp. 263–295). JAI Press.

Andrade, L. M., & Lundberg, C. A. (2018). The function to serve: A social-justice-oriented investigation of community college mission statements. *Journal of Hispanic Higher Education, 17*(1), 61–75. https://doi.org/10.1177/1538192716653503

Arellano Jr., L., Cuellar, M. G., & Gonzalez, A. M. (2022). Accountability to whom? Reimagining Hispanic Serving Institutions' financial models. *New Directions for Higher Education, 2022*(198), 87–99. https://doi.org/10.1002/he.20441

Baca, I., Hinojosa, Y. I., & Wolff Murphy, S. (2019). *Bordered writers: Latinx identities and literacy practices at Hispanic-Serving Institutions.* SUNY Press.

Benítez, M. (1998). Hispanic-Serving Institutions: Challenges and opportunities. *New Directions for Higher Education, 1998*(102), 57–68.

Bensimon, E. M., Dowd, A. C., Stanton-Salazar, R., & Dávila, B. A. (2019). The role of institutional agents in providing institutional support to Latinx students in STEM. *The Review of Higher Education*, *42*(4), 1689–1721. https://doi.org/10.1353/rhe.2019.0080

Boland, W. C. (2018). The Higher Education Act and Minority Serving Institutions: Towards a typology of Title III and V funded programs. *Education Sciences, 8*(33). https://doi.org/10.3390/educsci8010033

brown, a. m. (2017). *Emergent strategy: Shaping change, changing worlds.* AK Press.

Cataño, Y., & González, A. (2021). Examining *servingness* at California community college Hispanic-Serving Institutions (HSIs) for LGBTQ+ Latinx students. *Journal of the Alliance for Hispanic Serving Institution Educators, 1*(1), 55–72.

Comeaux, E., Grummert, S. E., & Cruz, N. (2021). Strategies of resistance among racially minoritized students at a Hispanic-Serving Institution: A critical race theory perspective. *Journal of Higher Education, 92*(3), 465–498. https://doi.org/10.1080/00221546.2020.1851569

Contreras, F. E. (2017). Latino faculty in Hispanic-Serving Institutions: Where is the diversity? *Association of Mexican American Educators Journal, 11*(3), 223–250. https://amaejournal.utsa.edu/index.php/AMAE/article/view/82

Contreras, F. E., Malcom, L. E., & Bensimon, E. M. (2008). Hispanic-Serving Institutions: Closeted identity and the production of equitable outcomes for Latina/o students. In M. Gasman, B. Baez, & C. S. T. Turner (Eds.), *Understanding minority-serving institutions* (pp.71–90). SUNY Press.

Covarrubias, R., Vasquez, A., Moreno, R., Estrada, J., Valle, I., & Zuñiga, K. (2020). Engaging families to foster holistic success of low income, Latinx first generation students at a Hispanic Serving Institution (HSI). In G. A. Garcia (Ed.), *Hispanic Serving Institutions (HSIs) in practice: Defining "servingness" at HSIs* (pp. 313–336). Information Age Publishing.

Cramblet Alvarez, L. D., Beeton, R. P., Saenz, C. N., & Schell, B. L. A. (2023). Redesigning the HSI curricular experience: Moving from Hispanic enrolling to Hispanic serving. *Journal of Latinos and Education, 22*(4), 1538–1547. https://doi.org/10.1080/15348431.2021.1998900

Cristobal, N., Johnston-Guerrero, M. P., & Garcia, G. A. (2021). Further contextualizing racial identity: Multiracial students at Hispanic Serving Institutions (HSIs). *Journal Committed to Social Change on Race and Ethnicity, 7*(2), 32–68. https://doi.org/10.15763/issn.2642-2387.2021.7.2.32-68

Cruz, C., Rajpal, G., Lecocke, M., Martines, I., & Lurie, A. (2021). Peer coaching program development: A framework of first-year Latina/o student persistence pursuing STEM pathways at a Hispanic Serving Institution. *Journal of Hispanic Higher Education, 20*(4), 365–384. https://doi.org/10.1177/1538192719867096

Cuellar, M., Segundo, V., & Muñoz, Y. (2017). Assessing empowerment at HSIs: An adapted inputs-environments-outcomes model. *Association of Mexican American Educators Journal, 11*(3), 84–108. https://amaejournal.utsa.edu/index.php/AMAE/article/view/76

Delgado Bernal, D. (1998). Using a Chicana feminist epistemology in educational research. *Harvard Educational Review, 68*(4), 555–582.

Desai, S. R., & Abeita, A. (2017). Institutional microaggressions at a Hispanic Serving Institution: A Diné (Navajo) woman utilizing Tribal Critical Race Theory through student activism. *Equity & Excellence in Education, 50*(3), 275–289. https://doi.org/10.1080/10665684.2017.1336498

DeTurk, S., & Briscoe, F. (2020). From equity and enlightenment to entrepreneurialism: An HSI's pursuit of "tier-one" status in the neoliberal era. *Review of Higher Education, 43*(4), 967–988. https://doi.org/10.1353/rhe.2020.0027

Doran, E. E. (2015). Negotiating access and tier one aspirations: The historical evolution of a striving Hispanic-Serving Institution. *Journal of Hispanic Higher Education, 14*(4), 343–354. https://doi.org/10.1177/1538192715570638
Doran, E., & Medina, Ø. (2017). The intentional and the grassroots Hispanic-Serving Institutions: A critical history of two universities. *Association of Mexican American Educators Journal, 11*(3), 29–49. https://amaejournal.utsa.edu/index.php/AMAE/article/view/74
Excelencia in Education. (n.d.). *Seal of Excelencia*. Retrieved December 12, 2025, from https://www.edexcelencia.org/seal-excelencia
Excelencia in Education. (2010). *Emerging Hispanic-Serving Institutions: Serving Latino students*. Excelencia in Education.
Excelencia in Education. (2024). *Emerging Hispanic-Serving Institutions (eHSIs): 2022–2023*. Excelencia in Education.
Flores, A., & Leal, D. R. (2023). Beyond enrollment and graduation: Examining strategic plans from Hispanic-Serving Institutions in Texas. *Journal of Latinos and Education, 22*(2), 454–469. https://doi.org/10.1080/15348431.2020.1791121
Franco, M. A., & Muñiz, C. M. (2022). Centering servingness: Framework-informed assessment of Hispanic-Serving Institutions. *New Directions for Student Services, 2022*(178–179), 97–109. https://doi.org/10.1002/ss.20432
Freire, P. (2014). *Pedagogy of the oppressed.* (30th Anniversary Edition). Bloomsbury Academic.
Garcia, G. A. (2017a). Defined by outcomes or culture? Constructing an organizational identity for Hispanic-Serving Institutions. *American Educational Research Journal*, 54(1S), 111S–134S. https://doi.org/10.3102/0002831216669779
Garcia, G. A. (2017b). What does it mean to be Latinx-serving? Testing the utility of the Typology of HSI Organizational Identities. *Association of Mexican American Educators Journal, 11*(3), 109–138. https://amaejournal.utsa.edu/index.php/AMAE/article/view/77/69
Garcia, G. A. (2018). Decolonizing Hispanic-Serving Institutions: A framework for organizing. *Journal of Hispanic Higher Education, 17*(2), 132–147. https://doi.org/10.1177/1538192717734289
Garcia, G. A. (2019). *Becoming Hispanic-Serving Institutions: Opportunities for colleges and universities*. Johns Hopkins University Press.
Garcia, G. A. (2019, December). *Defining "servingness" at Hispanic-Serving Institutions (HSIs): Practical implications for HSI leaders*. American Council on Education. https://www.equityinhighered.org/resources/ideas-and-insights/defining-servingness-at-hispanic-serving-institutions-hsis-practical-implications-for-hsi-leaders/
Garcia, G. A. (2020). *Hispanic Serving Institutions (HSIs) in practice: Defining "servingness" at HSIs*. Information Age Publishing.
Garcia, G. A. (2020, May). *Is liberation a viable outcome for students who attend college?* HigherEdJobs. https://bit.ly/3qHmAB1
Garcia, G. A. (2021). A love letter to HSI grant seekers/implementers and the federal agencies that fund them: Defining servingness in research, practice, & policy. *Journal of the Alliance for Hispanic Serving Institution Educators, 1*(1), 1–14.

Garcia, G. A. (Host). (2022, November 7). Leading and enacting servingness con cariño (No. 109) [Audio podcast episode]. In *¿Qué pasa, HSIs?*. https://www.ginaanngarcia.com/podcast/episode/a17dc1c6/leading-and-enacting-servingness-con-carino
Garcia, G. A. (2023). *Transforming Hispanic-Serving Institutions for Equity & Justice*. Johns Hopkins University Press.
Garcia, G. A. (Host). (2023, September 24). Embodying servingness: UCR Chicano Student Programs (No. 303) [Audio podcast episode]. In *¿Qué pasa, HSIs?*. https://www.ginaanngarcia.com/podcast/episode/966a6021/embodying-servingness-ucr-chicano-student-programs
Garcia, G. A. (Host). (2023, October 22). Spaces of empowerment: HSI student equipos (No. 307) [Audio podcast episode]. In *¿Qué pasa, HSIs?*. https://www.ginaanngarcia.com/podcast/episode/a03adfcb/spaces-of-empowerment-hsi-student-equipos
Garcia, G. A. (2023, November 20). *The HSI Movement will not be televised*. Dr. Gina Ann Garcia. https://www.ginaanngarcia.com/post/the-hsi-movement-will-not-be-televised
Garcia, G. A. (Host). (2024, January 28). Honoring the past & strategizing for the future (No. 401) [Audio podcast episode]. In *¿Qué pasa, HSIs?*. https://www.ginaanngarcia.com/podcast/episode/abeaa38d/honoring-the-past-and-strategizing-for-the-future
Garcia, G. A. (2024, September 9). *Becoming an unapologetic HSI*. Dr. Gina Ann Garcia. https://www.ginaanngarcia.com/post/becoming-an-unapologetic-hsi
Garcia, G. A. (Host). (2024, October 6). ¿Si no yo, quien? HSI directors leading the way (No. 505) [Audio podcast episode]. In *¿Qué pasa, HSIs?*. https://www.ginaanngarcia.com/podcast/episode/99ad0319/si-no-yo-quien-hsi-directors-leading-the-way
Garcia, G. A., & Cuellar, M. G. (2023). Advancing "intersectional servingness" in research, practice, and policy with Hispanic-Serving Institutions. *AERA Open*, *9*. https://doi.org/10.1177/23328584221148421
Garcia, G. A., Kim, H., Santos, N. J., & Meza, A. (2025). Influences on organizational identity development in the context of Hispanic-Serving Institutions (HSIs). In L. W. Perna (Ed.), *Higher education: Handbook of theory and research*. Springer Nature. https://doi.org/10.1007/978-3-031-86738-5_3-1
Garcia, G. A., & Morgan, D. L. (2025). Mission-based vs. enrollment-based institutions: Segmented governance at a Catholic Hispanic Serving Institution (HSI). *Review of Higher Education*, *49*(1), 1–32. https://doi.org/10.1353/rhe.0.a952249
Garcia, G. A., Núñez, A.-M., & Sansone, V. A. (2019a). Toward a multidimensional conceptual framework for understanding "servingness" in Hispanic-Serving Institutions (HSIs): A synthesis of the research. *Review of Educational Research*, *89*(5), 745–784. https://doi.org/10.3102/0034654319864591
Garcia, G. A., & Okhidoi, O. (2015). Culturally relevant practices that "serve" students at a Hispanic Serving Institution. *Innovative Higher Education*, *40*(4), 345–357. https://doi.org/10.1007/s10755-015-9318-7

Garcia, G. A., & Ramirez, J. J. (2018). Institutional agency at a Hispanic Serving Institution (HSI): Using social capital to empower students. *Urban Education, 53*(3), 355–381. https://doi.org/10.1177/0042085915623341
Garcia, G. A., Ramirez, J. J., Patrón, O. E., & Cristobal, N. L. (2019b). Constructing an HSI organizational identity at three Hispanic-Serving Institutions in the Midwest: Ideal versus current identity. *Journal of Higher Education, 90*(4), 513–538. https://doi.org/10.1080/00221546.2018.1522198
Garcia, G. A., & Zaragoza, M. (2020). Students' perceptions of diversity at two Hispanic-Serving Institutions through pictures: A focus on structures for serving. *Association of Mexican American Educators Journal, 14*(3), 10–29. https://doi.org/10.24974/amae.14.3.388
González, A. D. J., & Cataño, Y. (2020). Queering community college HSIs: An environmental scan of current programs and services for Latinx students. *Journal of Applied Research in the Community College, 27*(1), 74–88.
Griffin-Fennell, F. D., & Lerner, J. E. (2020). Professional development for faculty and staff at a Hispanic Serving Institution. In G. A. Garcia (Ed.), *Hispanic Serving Institutions (HSIs) in practice: Defining "servingness" at HSIs* (pp. 61–77). Information Age Publishing.
Hagedorn, L. S. (2007). The academic legacy of Berta Vigil Laden. *Community College Review, 35*(2), 147–154. https://doi.org/10.1177/0091552107306417
Hagedorn, L. S., & Cepeda, R. (2004). Serving Los Angeles: Urban community colleges and educational success among Latino students. *Community College Journal of Research and Practice, 28*(3), 199–211. https://doi.org/10.1080/10668920490256390
Hatch, M. J., & Schultz, M. (2002). The dynamics of organizational identity. *Human Relations, 55*(8), 989–1018. https://doi.org/10.1177/0018726702055008181
Hayes, K., & Kaba, M. (2023). *Let this radicalize you: Organizing and the revolution of reciprocal care*. Haymarket Books.
Hispanic Association of Colleges and Universities (HACU). (2024). *2024 HACU legislative agenda*. https://www.hacu.net/images/hacu/Newsrel/2024/2024_HACULegislativeAgenda.pdf
hooks, b. (1994). *Teaching to transgress: Education as the practice of freedom*. Routledge.
Imarisha, W., & brown, a. m. (Eds.). (2015). *Octavia's brood: Science fiction stories from social justice movements*. AK Press.
Kato, E. B., & Marinez, E. R. (2020). Defining servingness through learning communities: Sense of belonging for Latinx STEM transfer students at an HSI. In G. A. Garcia (Ed.), *Hispanic Serving Institutions (HSIs) in practice: Defining "servingness" at HSIs* (pp. 253–274). Information Age Publishing.
Kezar, A. (2009). Change in higher education: Not enough, or too much? *Change: The Magazine of Higher Learning, 41*(6), 18–23.
Kezar, A. (2010). Faculty and staff grassroots leaders' beliefs about power: Do their beliefs affect their strategies and effectiveness. *International Journal of Leadership Studies, 6*(1), 84–112.

Kezar, A. (2018). *How colleges change: Understanding, leading, and enacting change* (2nd ed.). Routledge.

Kezar, A., Bertram Gallant, T., & Lester, J. (2011). Everyday people making a difference on college campuses: The tempered grassroots leadership tactics of faculty and staff. *Studies in Higher Education, 36*(2), 129–151. https://doi.org/10.1080/03075070903532304

Kezar, A. J., & Eckel, P. (2002a). Examining the institutional transformation process: The importance of sensemaking, interrelated strategies, and balance. *Research in Higher Education, 43*(3), 295–328.

Kezar, A. J., & Eckel, P. (2002b). The effect of institutional culture on change strategies in higher education: Universal principles or culturally responsive concepts? *Journal of Higher Education, 73*(4), 435–460. https://doi.org/10.1080/00221546.2002.11777159

Kezar, A., Gehrke, S., & Bernstein-Sierra, S. (2018). Communities of transformation: Creating changes to deeply entrenched issues. *Journal of Higher Education, 89*(6), 832–864. https://doi.org/10.1080/00221546.2018.1441108

Kezar, A., Hallett, R. E., Corwin, Z. B., & Hypolite, L. (2025). Moving toward institutional culture change in higher education: An exploration into cross-functional professional learning communities. *Innovative Higher Education, 50*, 687–714. https://doi.org/10.1007/s10755-024-09753-1

Kezar, A. J., & Lester, J. (2009). *Organizing higher education for collaboration: A guide for campus leaders*. Jossey-Bass.

Kezar, A. J., & Lester, J. (2011). *Enhancing campus capacity for leadership: An examination of grassroots leaders in higher education*. Stanford University Press.

Kovats Sánchez, G. (2021). "If we don't do it, nobody is going to talk about it": Indigenous students disrupting Latinidad at Hispanic-serving institutions. *AERA Open, 7*(1), 1–13. https://doi.org/10.1177/23328584211059194

Laden, B. V. (1999). Two-year Hispanic-serving colleges. In B. K. Townsend (Ed.), *Two-year colleges for women and minorities* (pp. 151–194). Routledge.

Laden, B. V. (2001). Hispanic-serving institutions: Myths and realities. *Peabody Journal of Education, 76*(1), 73–92.

Laden, B. V. (2003). The role of Hispanic-serving colleges in the US system of higher education. In J. W. Guthrie (Ed.), *Encyclopedia of education* (2nd ed., Vol. 3, pp. 1045–1048). Macmillan Reference Library.

Laden, B. V. (2004a). Hispanic-serving institutions: What are they? Where are they? *Community College Journal of Research and Practice, 28*(3), 181–198. https://doi.org/10.1080/10668920490256381

Laden, B. V. (2004b). Introduction. *Community College Journal of Research and Practice, 28*(3), 177–180. https://doi.org/10.1080/10668920490256372

López, M., Cortés Maravilla, A., & Mercado-Lopez, L. M. (2020). The "Latin@s in Academia" lecture series: Testimonios as a tool for enhancing cultural validation, belongingness, and graduate school aspirations at an HSI. In G. A. Garcia (Ed.), *Hispanic Serving Institutions (HSIs) in practice: Defining "servingness" at HSIs* (pp. 275–293). Information Age Publishing.

Malcom-Piqueux, L., & Bensimon, E. M. (2015). Design principles for equity and excellence at Hispanic-Serving Institutions. *PERSPECTIVAS: Issues in Higher Education Policy and Practice*, 4, 1–16.

Marin, P., & Pereschica, P. (2017). Becoming an Hispanic-Serving Research Institution: Involving graduate students in organizational change. *Association of Mexican American Educators Journal*, *11*(3), 154–175. https://amaejournal.utsa.edu/index.php/AMAE/article/view/79

Masters, B. G., Beltran, E., & Rodriguez-Kiino, D. (2020). Academic mindset development at a Hispanic-Serving Institution: Using non-academic outcomes indicators of "serving" STEM students. In G. A. Garcia (Ed.), *Hispanic Serving Institutions (HSIs) in practice: Defining "servingness" at HSIs* (pp. 231–252). Information Age Publishing.

McDonnell, L. M., & Elmore, R. F. (1987). Getting the job done: Alternative policy instruments. *Educational Evaluation and Policy Analysis*, *9*(2), 133–152.

McNaughtan, J., & Lujan, J. (2023). "A moral, ethical, and fiduciary obligation to serve": Perceptions of the role of presidents at Hispanic-serving community colleges. *Community College Journal of Research and Practice*. Advance online publication. https://doi.org/10.1080/10668926.2023.2189179

Meyerson, D. E. (2001). *Tempered radicals: How everyday leaders inspire change at work*. Harvard Business School.

Meza, A. (2023). Pintando a Hispanic Serving Institution: The influence of muralism on Chicanx/Latinx student experience at the University of California HSI campuses. *Journal of Student Affairs*, *19*, 8–25. https://steinhardt.nyu.edu/sites/default/files/2023-05/JoSA-Volume19-FINAL.pdf

Miller, R. A., & Holliday-Millard, P. (2021). Debating diversity and social justice curricular requirements: How organizational culture at a liberal arts college informed the change process. *Journal of Higher Education*, *92*(7), 1085–1108. https://doi.org/10.1080/00221546.2021.1912553

Muñoz, M. (2009) In their own words and by the numbers: A mixed-methods study of Latina community college presidents. *Community College Journal of Research and Practice*, *34*(1–2), 153–174. https://doi.org/10.1080/10668920903385939

Núñez, A.-M. (2022) Creating cultures of student success: Insights from Hispanic-Serving Institution computer science departments. *Change: The Magazine of Higher Learning*, *54*(5), 44–51. https://doi.org/10.1080/00091383.2022.2101867

Núñez, A.-M. (2024). Toward opportunity-centered institutional logics: Evidence from Hispanic-Serving Institutions and science equity efforts. *Journal of Higher Education*. Advance online publication. https://doi.org/10.1080/00221546.2024.2344531

Nuñez, A.-M., & Bowers, A. J. (2011). Exploring what leads high school students to enroll in Hispanic-Serving Institutions: A multilevel analysis. *American Educational Research Journal*, *48*(6), 1286–1313. https://doi.org/10.3102/0002831211408061

O'Brien, E., & Zudak, C. (1998). Minority-Serving Institutions: An overview. *New Directions for Higher Education, 1998*(102), 5–15.
Olivas, M. (1982). Indian, Chicano, and Puerto Rican colleges: Status and issues. *Bilingual Review, 9*, 36–58.
Orphan, C. M., & Hartley, J. M. (2021). How change unravels: The failure of ideal-centered organizational change at regional comprehensive universities. *Journal of Higher Education, 92*(3), 385–409. https://doi.org/10.1080/00221546.2020.1809269
Ortega, G., Aguilar-Smith, S., & Lizalde, G. (2023). Barriers to power: Exploring the troubled trajectories of Latinx executive leaders at Hispanic-Serving Institutions. *Innovative Higher Education*. Advance online publication. https://doi.org/10.1007/s10755-023-09649-6
Pedersen, J. S., & Dobbin, F. (2006). In search of identity and legitimation: Bridging organizational culture and neoinstitutionalism. *American Behavioral Scientist, 49*(7), 897–907. https://doi.org/10.1177/0002764205284798
Perez, L. (2020). To what extent are Title V grants and educational expenditures associated with educational attainment of Latinxs at Hispanic-Serving Institutions? *Journal of Hispanic Higher Education, 19*(4), 323–334. https://doi.org/10.1177/1538192718801792
Perna, L. W., Li, C., Walsh, E., & Raible, S. (2010). The status of equity for Hispanics in public higher education in Florida and Texas. *Journal of Hispanic Higher Education, 9*(2), 145–166. https://doi.org/10.1177/1538192709331973
Petrov, L. A., & Garcia, G. A. (2021). Becoming a racially just Hispanic-Serving Institution (HSI): Leveraging HSI grants for organizational identity change. *Journal of Diversity in Higher Education*. http://dx.doi.org/10.1037/dhe0000356
Piñeda, D. (2010). *A federal intervention to improve Latino college participation: Evidence from the Title V developing Hispanic-serving institutions program* [Unpublished doctoral dissertation]. University of Michigan.
Pirtle, W. N., Brock, B., Aldonza, N., Leke, K., & Edge, D. (2021). "I didn't know what anti-Blackness was until I got here": The unmet needs of Black students at Hispanic-Serving Institutions. *Urban Education*. Advance online publication. https://doi.org/10.1177/00420859211044948
Ponjuán, L., Palomín, L., & Hernández, S. (2017). Presidential leadership: Improving completion rates of Latino male students at Texas community colleges. *Association of Mexican American Educators Journal, 11*(3), 178–198. https://amaejournal.utsa.edu/index.php/AMAE/article/view/80
Poza, L. E., Pinedo-Gangai, L., Barrera, M., Burciaga, R., & Pizarro, M. (2022). Making movidas: Cultivating leadership through conocimiento in an undergraduate student retreat. *Journal of Leadership, Equity, and Research, 8*(2). http://journals.sfu.ca/cvj/index.php/cvj/index
Quinteros, K. N., & Covarrubias, R. (2023). Reimagining leadership through the everyday resistance of faculty of color. *Journal of Diversity in Higher Education*. Advance online publication. https://dx.doi.org/10.1037/dhe0000471
Ritchie, A. J. (2023). *Practicing new worlds: Abolition and emergent strategies*. AK Press.

Roberts, S. A., & Lucas, K. L. (2022). A Title V center as a counterspace for underrepresented minority and first-generation college students. *Journal of Hispanic Higher Education, 21*(2), 198–211. https://doi.org/10.1177/1538192720951307

Sánchez Ordaz, A., Reguerín, P., & Sánchez, S. E. (2020). Theater to strengthen holistic advising at a Hispanic Serving Institution. In G. A. Garcia (Ed.), *Hispanic Serving Institutions (HSIs) in practice: Defining "servingness" at HSIs* (pp. 79–95). Information Age Publishing.

Santiago, D. A., Taylor, M., & Calderón Galdeano, E. (2016). *From capacity to success: HSIs, Title V, and Latino students*. Excelencia in Education.

Scott, B. L., Muñoz, S. M., & Scott, S. B. (2022). How whiteness operates at a Hispanic Serving Institution: A qualitative case study of faculty, staff, and administrators. *Journal of Diversity in Higher Education, 17*(4), 563–574. http://dx.doi.org/10.1037/dhe0000438

Solórzano, D. G. (1995). The baccalaureate origins of Chicana and Chicano doctorates in the social sciences. *Hispanic Journal of Behavioral Sciences, 17*(1), 3–32.

Solórzano, D. G., & Yosso, T. J. (2001). Critical race and LatCrit theory and method: Counter-storytelling. *International Journal of Qualitative Studies in Education, 14*(4), 471–495. https://doi.org/10.1080/09518390110063365

Solórzano, D. G., & Yosso, T. J. (2002). Critical race methodology: Counter-storytelling as an analytic framework for education research. *Qualitative Inquiry, 8*(1), 23–44.

Squire, D., & Liu, P. (2022). Learning from the past to create an equitable future: An archival study of a university emerging as a Hispanic-Serving Institution. *About Campus, 27*(1), 20–30. https://doi.org/10.1177/10864822221102956

Stanton-Salazar, R. D. (2011). A social capital framework for the study of institutional agents and their role in the empowerment of low-status students and youth. *Youth & Society, 43*, 1066–1109.

Tierney, W. G. (1988). Organizational culture in higher education: Defining the essentials. *Journal of Higher Education, 59*(1), 2–21.

US Department of Education. (n.d.). *How to determine institutional eligibility for titles III, V, and VII grants*. Office of Postsecondary Education. Retrieved December 12, 2025, from https://www2.ed.gov/about/offices/list/ope/idues/insteligcht.pdf

Valdez, P. L. (2015). An overview of Hispanic-Serving Institutions' legislation: Legislation policy formation between 1979 and 1992. In J. P. Mendez, I. F. A. Bonner, J. Méndez-Negrete, & R. T. Palmer (Eds.), *Hispanic-Serving Institutions in American higher education: Their origin, and present and future challenges* (pp. 5–29). Stylus.

Vargas, N., & Villa-Palomino, J. (2018). Racing to serve or race-ing for money? Hispanic-Serving Institutions and the colorblind allocation of racialized federal funding. *Sociology of Race and Ethnicity*, 1–15. https://doi.org/10.1177/2332649218769409

Vargas, N., Villa-Palomino, J., & Davis, E. (2019). Latinx faculty representation and resource allocation at Hispanic Serving Institutions. *Race Ethnicity and Education*, *23*(1), 39–54. https://doi.org/10.1080/13613324.2019.1679749
Velez, G., Black, J., López, S., & D'Anna-Hernandez, K. (2024). From predominantly white to Hispanic-Serving: Latinx student experiences on a campus in transition. *Journal of Hispanic Higher Education*, *23*(2), 73–87. https://doi.org/10.1177/15381927231161801
Venegas, E. M., Koonce, J. B., Lancaster, L., Bazan, J., & Garza, A. (2021). Diversifying the 'HSI bubble': Black and Asian women faculty at Hispanic-Serving Institutions. *Race Ethnicity and Education*, 1–20. https://doi.org/10.1080/13613324.2021.1924139
Villarreal, C. D. (2022). Servingness in the borderlands: A study of faculty hiring at a Hispanic-serving institution on the border. *AERA Open*, *8*(1), 1–12. https://doi.org/10.1177/23328584221099597
Villarreal Sosa, L., Garcia, G. A., & Bucher, J. (2023). Decolonizing faculty governance at Hispanic Serving Institutions. *Journal of Hispanic Higher Education*, 22(3), 325–341. https://doi.org/10.1177/15381927221126781
Weissman, S. (2025, June 13). *Tennessee lawsuit puts HSIs' fate on the line*. Inside Higher Ed. https://www.insidehighered.com/news/government/politics-elections/2025/06/13/tenn-lawsuit-puts-hispanic-servings-fate-line
Weissman, S. (2025, September 11). *Education Department moves to end funding for minority-serving institutions*. Inside Higher Ed. https://www.insidehighered.com/news/government/politics-elections/2025/09/11/education-department-moves-end-msi-programs
Whetten, D. A., & Mackey, A. (2002). A social actor conception of organizational identity and its implications for the study of organizational reputation. *Business Society*, *41*(4), 393–414. https://doi.org/10.1177/0007650302238775
Wolf-Wendel, L. E., Baker, D. B., & Morphew, C. C. (2000). Dollars and $ense: Institutional resources and the baccalaureate origins of women doctorates. *Journal of Higher Education*, *71*(2), 165–186.
Zaragoza, M., & Garcia, G. A. (2023). Latina faculty at a Catholic Hispanic-Serving Institution: Critical counter-stories about racialized & gendered experiences and servingness. *Journal of Higher Education*, *95*(4), 473–495. https://doi.org/10.1080/00221546.2023.2217740

INDEX